SCIENCE AND CULTURE SERIES
REV. JOSEPH HUSSLEIN, S.J., PH.D., GENERAL EDITOR

THE OXFORD MOVEMENT
1833 to 1933

1933

OXFORD

Oxford Town consoles my care
Dreaming of the Middle Ages there,
But Oxford has the Faith: appearance tends
That way at least: her jeweled Science ends in jewels
   precious, delicate.
The skies with prestige coronate
Study and Silence such as love requires,
While Wisdom recompenses mental spires.
That needful Wisdom, sweetly reasoning power,
Cathedral cutteth short at praying hour.

          (Translated from the French of Verlaine)

Of forms they talked that rose as if in joy
   Like magic isles from an enchanted foam,
They prophesied (no prophet like a boy)
   Some fairer Oxford and some freer Rome.

And Hail the hour, they cried, when each high morn
   England at one shall stand at the Church gate
And Vesper bells o'er all the land be borne
   And Newman mould the Church and Gladstone stamp
     the State!

       (From the *New Atlantis,* by Archbishop Alexander)

The
Oxford Movement
1833 - 1933

By SHANE LESLIE
M. A. King's College, Cambridge

Quaesivit coelo lucem ingemuitque reperta.
— Æneid, IV, 692.

THE BRUCE PUBLISHING COMPANY

MILWAUKEE

TO

CHARLES

NINTH DUKE OF MARLBOROUGH

PRINCE

OF THE HOLY ROMAN EMPIRE

PREFACE BY THE GENERAL EDITOR

Over three thousand volumes on the Oxford Movement are said to have issued from the press. With its centenary year the literary floodgates opened anew. To contribute merely another volume would be to add just another drop to the vast inundation.

And yet no apology is needed for the appearance of Mr. Leslie's book at this moment. As a piece of literature it occupies a place unique and apart by itself. It is the work of an artist no less than of an historian; of a writer intimately familiar with his theme and dealing with it at perfect ease, in serious vein or light. It is no mere collection of statistical data, but its sudden flashes of wit may often reveal to us more, in one vivid illumination, than might be gleaned from rows of learned tomes.

While due importance must be given to scholarly work of a more voluminous nature, the author's own choice, under existing circumstances, has been to apply the wise Shakespearian dictum, that brevity is the soul of wit. Yet, in spite of countless eliminations made with Spartan heroism, even in the already completed manuscript, he has succeeded in offering a remarkably comprehensive book, reviewing the entire Movement in its outstanding features, its inner spirit, and its lasting effects. His work will prove to be of equal interest to Anglican and Roman. It appeals to all.

The practical question, "Is the Oxford Movement dead, or is it still a vital issue?" may here perhaps present itself to the mind of the reader. In answer, let us first distinguish between the Movement itself and its effects. As a Movement, we can readily concede that it has spent its force. In its effects, it continues to-day and will remain living and active for generations to come.

Anglicanism itself, despite its almost entire spectrum of beliefs that vary from an all but pure Catholicism down to the ultimate shades of Modernism, has yet genuinely benefitted by the Oxford Movement. New forces are to-day perpetuating some of its earlier aspirations, although true directive energy may often have been lost. It was the Romeward trend alone, let us not forget, which gave its great *élan* to the Oxford Movement. With this gone the nature of that Movement was changed and it ceased to exist. But the Romeward trend itself did not for that reason pass away from within the Church of England. We know that it still exists.

To appreciate, on the other hand, what this Movement has permanently meant for the ancient Church in the land that once was Mary's Dower, we need only finger, quite at random, any of the pages of an English *Catholic Who's Who*. It may surprise us to discover the long list of distinguished men and women after whose names is recorded briefly the date of their reception into the Church. Singly or in groups they were welcomed back to the arms of the Great Mother whence centuries ago their forefathers had wandered in the days that tried men's hearts. And all this, it should be noted, had been effected with comparatively little effort or intervention on the part of the Church, Catholic and Roman, which most abundantly reaped the rich harvests of the Oxford Movement, not in England only, but in all the English-speaking countries.

A single century thus sufficed to bring about the inception, development, and final passing away of this Movement, one of the most significant and important recorded in modern times, an event almost epic in its nature, with its clash of thought, its high-resounding words, and ceaseless brunt of conflicts carried on triumphantly under the leadership of one who ultimately took the last, logical, and decisive step — the rendering of spiritual fealty to Rome, a step never retracted and never regretted on his part.

The Oxford Movement, as Mr. Leslie conceives of it, was primarily and mainly Anglican. It began within the Church of England and was enthusiastically developed within her halls of learning by her most brilliant and progressive thinkers. Out of the inertia of a dormant Anglicanism it arose, culminated in the fearless and magnificent challenge of the Romeward Movement, and then slowly sank to its decline, passing into history before the relentless force of an insurgent Modernism. Within the Church of England there was now none left to shout, "To thy tents, O Israel!" But the Movement has served its providential purpose.

If Newman was the outstanding leader to make his submission and enter into communion with the See of Peter, he was followed, singly and in turn, by a large number of Oxford's noble and illustrious sons. Cambridge, too, her sister university, gave its royal quota. There was no flaunting of banners, no fanfare of trumpets, as these men went forth, solemnly, resolutely, following the voice of their conscience, and not seldom at the cost of heroic sacrifices. But the peace they found was worth all that they gave.

It is the story of this Movement and its effects which Mr. Leslie tells in his own inimitable way, with a wealth of intimate information, felicitous anecdotes, and literary amenities, which will render it one of the most interesting and original contributions to a great theme.

JOSEPH HUSSLEIN, S.J., PH.D.,
General Editor, Science and Culture Series.

St. Louis University,
April 12, 1933.

CONTENTS

		PAGE
OXFORD		iv
PREFACE BY THE GENERAL EDITOR		x
LIST OF ILLUSTRATIONS		xv
THE OXFORD MOVEMENT		1
PRELUDE		6
I.	THE SEED-BED OF THE PAST	13
II.	THE FIRST PHASE	39
III.	THE SECOND PHASE	68
IV.	THE PRESENT PHASE	111

APPENDIX

I.	UNPUBLISHED POEM BY NEWMAN	129
II.	IRELAND AND THE OXFORD MOVEMENT	133
III.	RELIGIOUS ORDERS IN THE CHURCH OF ENGLAND	139
IV.	THE OXFORD MOVEMENT IN ARCHITECTURE	144
V.	THE OXFORD MOVEMENT IN LITERATURE	150
VI.	THE REACTION ON THE CATHOLIC CHURCH IN ENGLAND	165
VII.	A SELECT BIBLIOGRAPHY OF THE OXFORD MOVEMENT	183
VIII.	MAP OF THE OXFORD MOVEMENT	190

ILLUSTRATIONS

JOHN HENRY CARDINAL NEWMAN . . . *facing page 49*

JOHN KEBLE . . . . *facing page 65*

DR. EDWARD B. PUSEY . . . . *facing page 80*

HENRY EDWARD CARDINAL MANNING . . *facing page 96*

THE OXFORD MOVEMENT

The Oxford Movement attained its Centenary in July, 1933. It is the only intellectual movement England has ever bred. It was original of England as the Renaissance was of Italy, the Reformation of Germany, and the Revolution of France. This sketch offers a skeleton key to the Movement, which in turn is a pass-key to the Victorian Era. The Oxford Movement proved more than a shaking of dry bones. It was a sudden ripening of varied fruit on a vine that seemed barren. Its first phase rose out of the core of the Church of England. It was Anglican but anti-Roman and anti-Protestant at once. It was single-aimed and single-minded and led by a single leader in a Catholic direction. The second phase opened when Newman seceded to Rome and the force of the Catholic revival was divided into twin channels: the Anglo-Catholic flood in the national Church and the Roman Restoration in an English backwater. On the one hand, as Gladstone sadly wrote, were "some of the most gifted sons reared by Oxford for the service of the Church of England hurling at her head the hottest bolts of the Vatican." On the other hand, Newman claimed that the ancient Catholic Church in England had received her Second Spring. The spirit of revival and restoration passed like a quickening gale through both religious communities. Such was the ecclesiastical side of the Oxford Movement. The bibliography of the Movement includes over a thousand Theologies, Lives, Memoirs, Pamphlets, and books of controversy. It is impossible to do more than throw out a spate of suggestion and anecdote in so slight a volume as this, which is intended to touch the historical founts as well as the many currents of that fascinating reversion in English Religion and Thought.

The Movement was not merely a religious awakening. It was welcomed by such a thinker as Mill because it stirred Thought on other sides. Antagonisms and antipathies were created. Within and without the Church of England there commenced that mode of treating ancient sanctities which has ended in the familiar Modernism. At Oxford the Modernist descent may be traced under such names as Germanising, Liberal, Broad Church. Likewise the High Churchmen passed through the stages of Tractarian, Puseyite, and Ritualist before they became generally accepted as Anglo-Catholics. To save confusion it is best to use the word Roman or Roman Catholic of the Universal Church in a treatise such as this, for the word remains the only thing Anglicans have not yet borrowed. Parallel with the Roman Revival in England arose the great sceptical movement also called Rationalist and Agnostic. Newman made hundreds believe but he caused thousands to think. Not all thought aright. Huxley claimed that he could compose a Sceptical Catechism out of his writings. Newman was sceptical of Anglican assumptions, but not of the truth when this had become clear to him. The pressure upon men at Oxford made

them think, and Thought for a time led to Rome or nowhere. Those who remained in the Church of England
continued either on religious or agnostic lines and the two
groups survive under the same roof until to-day.

Thought engenders Thought and beauty awakens
beauty. The Oxford Movement vitalised the dead Gothic
Revival. Parallel to the Gothic architects led by Pugin
arose the art-writers led by Ruskin. Research for primitive
theology led to desire for primitive painting and the Pre-
Raphaelites took their being. The restoration of Catholic
churches led to revivals of the mediæval Guild and William Morris took his place beside Ruskin at Oxford. Both
tended towards that Socialism which is mediæval Catholicism turned inside out. On the one side of them germinated the English Labour Movement and on the other
the æsthetic Movement of Pater and Wilde. Betwixt and
between came the Christian Socialism of the High
Church. The Oxford Movement must not be made responsible for more than it genuinely inspired, but when
not the actual seed it was often the phosphate fertilizing
the fallow field. Apart from controversies about ritual and
doctrine, there is hardly a corner of English intellectual
life, which it failed to touch. Architecture it wholly ab-
sorbed for a time together with all the arts and crafts of
builder and decorator. From Church buildings the im-
print passed to secular constructions. The impress on literature was enormous, especially when it is remembered
that during the first part of the Victorian Era Theology
led the book trade. Novels, poetry, history were no less affected by stirrings and ripples of the Oxford Movement,

whether as propaganda, appreciation, or definite opposition. There was hardly a corner of the national life or a family in the educated classes untouched one way or another. While the High Church made a noble bid for the allegiance of the English poor, the Romeward movement took tribute of almost every noble family in the three Kingdoms. Few of the Stately Homes of England did not yield a convert even in the humble ranks of cousinhood. The Ritualists set out to win the slum-dwellers on lines of Christian Socialism. The Roman Church in Britain found its poor ready-made in the Irish. The Oxford Movement in devious ways expended its evangelic force into the two Churches, which challenge each other in English life. Whether either of them can to-day challenge the English nation is a different, perhaps a doubtful, tale.

With the Centenary a certain historical interest arises. The Oxford Movement was one of the galvanising sparks which set the minds of Victorians alight to their own intense satisfaction and to the amusement of their descendants. All the names attached to the Movement from the great Churchmen like Newman, Manning, Pusey, and Wilberforce to Pugin, Ruskin, Pater, and Wilde, who without exception may be accounted its camp-followers, have yielded a harvest to the talents and sometimes to the talons of modern biographers.

But the deeper motives and the secret founts from which they drank often escape the biographers of their fame and still more those who play skittles with the idiosyncrasies of the great. The interest of the Oxford Movement is often one of contrast. The Victorians were too great for their age. To-day it is the reverse and the Age engulfs those who struggle to the surface of the waters. The contrast is too fierce to be pleasant. Of what avail to mock the Victorians, who disdain us from the Olympian heights of their honesty, seriousness, sincerity, and, most impregnable of all, their serenity. We avenge ourselves by laughing at people who fought desperately for a surplice or a vestment, made tragedies over lit candles, and gave commonplace things the values of eternity. Conversions to Rome or Anglo-Catholic triumphs no longer fascinate or anger the public. They mean nothing in an England which will only listen to the daring outspeech of Modernists in high places. The Oxford Movement may be dead, but let the Centenary be an honourable carrying out to burial.

PRELUDE

Oxford a hundred years ago was nearer the times of
Elizabeth than modern Oxford to the days of Newman
and Manning, Pusey and Gladstone. Like Rome, Oxford
was a mediæval City living behind her walls with fields
sweeping her like a green Campagna. Cities then stayed
still and lived their inner life. The modern cosmopolis,
which grows like a wen or a fungus until it collapses
under its own statistics, was undreamed, nor would it
have been considered an improvement. Cities were pleasant dreams in which to wander by day, not the inextri-
cable nightmare of the present. Oxford, like Rome, lay
wrapped in her past. No railway had dared to approach
either and the chief commerce of either town with the
outer world was one of clerics and students. The old Dons
at Oxford and the venerable Cardinals in Rome would
have shuddered in their libraries or upon their pleasant
garden walks, had they foreseen the throne of the Popes
made the screaming Capital of a fighting modern Power,
of the Seminary of Addison, Gibbon, and Dr. Johnson
turned into a centre of motor industry. Rome knelt at the
ever-burning lamps on the tombs of the Apostles, while
the Oxford Colleges, like the foolish virgins, slept with
lamps unlit and their pious founders unentreated in
prayer. The Church of England had occupied her old
buildings since the flight of James II. Strange to say there

was still one man living, the President of Magdalen, Dr. Routh, approaching his centenary, who had sat in the lap of old Dr. Hough, who as a Scholar of Magdalen had been actually expelled by the last of the Stuart Kings in 1688. Routh lived to see Newman come to Oxford and go.

These were the memories of Oxford in the 'Thirties. Of her pinnacles and spires wrapped in the noiseless beauty of the Middle Ages who will care to speak to-day? No doubt she had reached that stage of decrepid certitude in things most questionable, which is not far removed from stagnation. Legitimate doubts, which are the stepping-stones to progress, did not occur. Parties and partisans there were none. Oxford housed a great society of Anglicans, some of whom may have signed the Articles with a smile or a sigh, but saw no reason for intruding on the good feeling and fellowship of others. There was a High-and-Dry Church in possession not only of the Universities but of the Bishoprics and the most of the rich benefices. They were not High in any modern sense. Still less were they Dry as we use that term. They lived without ideal, which is far more dangerous than to cherish a lost cause or passionate crusade.

Yet it had not been always so. There had been Jacobites and Nonjurors amongst them in the memory of men. The great Revolution of 1688 was not the first to sweep over University and land. But it had been serious and strong enough to lay the foundations of modern England and to discolour as well as shape the Church. Under the Protestant House of Hanover the Church became Whig and Erastian; in other words, it grovelled to the State. It was only in the recesses of Oxford that she pretended that she was Catholic and Tory and drank Jacobite healths. The Nonjurors and Jacobites and Roman Catholics were outcast in the land. Even in Oxford the Stuart memory died down and no Dons were willing to drink the King's health and confusion to the Pretender even with the famous aside:

> "But which is King and which Pretender,
> Ah, that no doubt is quite another thing."

The Nonjurors were true to the Church of England, but some of the Jacobites had been waiting to see which side the cat would jump and for their benefit an equivocal rhyme was used which Hearne the Nonjuror preserved in his papers.

It can be read in a different sense across or downward and by a curious irony might have served the New Prayer Book of 1928:

"I hold as faith   what England's Church allows
What Rome's Church
    saith   my conscience disavows
Where King is head   the Church can have no shame
The flock's misled   which holds the Pope supreme
Where altars dressed   your service's scarce divine
The people's blest   whose table's bread and wine
He's but an Ass   who the Communion flies
Who shuns the Mass   is Catholic and wise."

Catholic, of course, here carries two senses and is the source of confusion in writing of the Oxford Movement or Catholic Revival. It may mean either Roman, or else Catholic in that wide sense in which the Church of Eng-

land applies this word to the three Catholic Creeds outside communion with the Pope. The whole Oxford Movement was one long dispute as to the meaning of that word,
upon which men staked their souls or careers.

The historical trouble was that Oxford had once been
Roman. The most decisive point in the history of modern
Europe was when England slipped the Pope. Rome had
not understood that England would be of greater import
than Spain. The mystics perhaps had some such feeling
when they christened her "Our Lady's Dowry." England
not only picked up the balance of Europe but developed
an Empire and a Church. To-day as a result the sun presumably never sets on Pan-Anglicanism. The British Empire is Roman to-day so far as it is leavened by the Irish.
Had the English bided the Pope, a hundred Bishops' Sees
and a seventh of the globe might now acknowledge the
Papal Supremacy under the British Flag. If the Reformation in England turned on so small a pivot as a foiled
Divorce and the King's desire to make his harlot his
Queen, no slighter event has ever led to greater. But there
were other and long-growing and deep-implanted roots
to the Reformation for God's Englishmen.

They may be summarised. English folk, whether Saxon
or Norman, were not seldom anti-clericals in the Middle
Ages. For illustration of this it is only necessary to read
the fierce indictment of Piers Plowman. It is one side of
the shield. Saints, Mystics, and Contemplatives were few
in any days. Martyrs on either side were fewer still. The
peasant loved the shelter of the great Abbeys, but the
Lords were envious of Italian prelates who drew monies

from England. Rome, the centre of the Catholic Society
and the earthly Bride of Christ, was played to political
ambition. The folk had their Faith stolen because their
Lords were jealous of Rome. Even so the stubborn English
folk had made the Catholic idea practical, built the greatest set of national Cathedrals in Europe, given their hero-
worship to Thomas of Canterbury, prayed for a thousand
years at the Mass, danced round the Maypole, struggled
and suffered and muddled through under the shadow of
the Cross. But when the King bade them throw out the
Pope, enough were willing to start the gradual landslide.
Few of them realised what they were doing until it became a clean sweep in the end. The Oxford Movement
was an attempt to turn that landslide uphill again.

The incomprehensible fact of to-day is that England
could ever have been Roman or that Oxford was Roman
once. It is only the mediæval buildings, the relics of the
past, which enable the historian to trust his own documents. Over the portal of every College in Oxford the
mournful legend might be written: *Roma fuit!* There
Rome had been and gone. To spite the Pope the Church
of England defaced her own face.

Although the parish churches now carry the woeful
gloss of the restorer, a hundred years ago far more evidence of the old religion lay behind the broken boards
and dirty whitewash. Holy-water stoups filled with dust,
broken sedilia and Easter sepulchres made a refuge for
bottles or stands for hats, while the tombs of Crusaders
and benevolent Dames slept in alabaster inviting the
pocket knives of the careless. Here and there a Sanct-Bell

Cot housed bats, while the stubs of a Screen or a stepless Rood-stair testified to a lost story of English Art. Upon patined bronze were inscriptions imploring prayers for the dead. Mediæval memorials had been overbuilt by Georgian monuments and epitaphs which have been described as "everything that was haughty and worldly, faithless and heretical, irreverent, jocose and ridiculous." Instead of St. John and St. Mary weeping beneath the Rood, ghastly cherubs and blousy angels in marble invited attention to the pretended virtues of the deceased. Heavy-drinking Squires faced eternity in the garb of classical Emperors or enveloped themselves with togas as though emerging from the seclusion of a Turkish Bath. Dickens described the Churchyards as they were and parodied the pompous epitaph of "Ethelinda Reverential wife of Mr. Thomas Sapsea."

When the Victorian restorers began to clean the plant of the Establishment, they accomplished as much harm as the Italians who cleared the Colosseum of the Flora of centuries. But both revealed the stone-witness of a Rome which was no more. English life kept fascinating under-traces of the old. In folklore, St. Thomas and the Virgin were richly remembered. Superstitions lingered as perversions of the ancient Faith in remote Counties where her Sacraments were extinct. There had been quick transformations. The popular Flora stayed Catholic in a hundred instances. St. Edmund's Pool or Lane was often changed to Deadman's. St. Thomas the Apostle became quickly possessed of those devoted to the martyred Archbishop. The Scotch still ran the races dedicated to St. Mary's Mass on the Feast of the Assumption. Jarrow preserved the chair of one whom all England called Venerable, as that of "Admiral Bede"! There were a thousand relics for the antiquarian and ecclesiologist to recover. Two scenes will always illustrate the natural and perhaps not malicious irreverence that covered the land: Byron digging up the skull of the Abbot of Newstead to use as a drinking cup; and the authorities at Reading placing the great relic of the Abbey between two stuffed fish in a Museum, labelled "the Hand of St. James!" Was not this "arm of St. James" the oath of that great uncanonised Simon de Montfort before the Battle of Evesham? But with the old religion the mediæval culture of Englishmen passed away as though it had never been. The English could no longer understand how visible things could smack of the unseen or material things possibly become sacred. The Utilitarian superseded the mystical in "God's Englishmen." In the Middle Ages there was a macabre Dance of Death painted at St. Paul's Cathedral. It was left to Victorian England, said Gladstone in a rare burst of humour, to give a Parochial Ball to provide a certain Parish with a hearse! Ecclesiastical England, which had alluded to herself as "Our Lady's Dowry," a phrase redolent of the living Queen of Heaven, passed under the more practical instrument of Queen Anne's Bounty. The supremely sad symbol of the change came with those Puritans who hacked down the Holy Thorn of Glastonbury, which legend said Joseph of Arimathæa brought from Palestine. Was Jack and the Beanstalk, however practical, a better exchange in the minds of English children?

I

THE SEED-BED OF THE PAST

To the pious New Zealander or the Rhodes Scholar from Minnesota who paces the throbbing High Street of Oxford to-day, its Movement will coincide with the up-roar of noise and traffic. Only by penetrating cobbled lanes or nooks of College Gardens or by frequenting the corners of discreet and panelled Common rooms will he find re-pose to enquire or receive answer to his question: What was the Oxford Movement?

The Oxford Movement is a hundred years old. What is the reckoning of that century? It was connected closely with preceding centuries and its light is not yet dimmed by the advancing sand-storms of futurity. It was not an isolated chapter in English Church history. It does not read like the chart of a dried-up sea. Nor was it a mere by-blow in the great breeze of man's unconquerable thought. The Oxford Movement was the first and only time that England seemed to turn definitely on her tracks. It was a moment of transition after the Napoleonic wars, when educated Englishmen were deciding whether to be romantic or scientific. Ordinary folk had no choice but to become industrious under an industrial age.

It was a deliberate turning back of the clock when men wistfully recalled mediæval time and even tampered with works made in the Sixteenth Century, when England had broken from the Pope and the Holy Roman Empire as far as both presented a United Christendom. It was the all-important event of that century for England to set up an Anglican Church and a British Empire of her own. Her Empire has survived the Holy Roman, but her Church should not have passed the span of three hundred years in which the most lively and powerful of Heresies are said ordinarily to live and die. But the third Centenary of King Henry's break with Rome, in 1534, found the Church of England living, while that of the Elizabethan Settlement found her enjoying an unexpected revival. What had happened during the Victorian Era to avert decay and frustrate her doom? The answer is the Oxford Movement. The majestic, old, half-crumbling, giant-branched and water-logged English oaktree had thrown out a new leafage to her own amazement and was even enjoying a burst of fruit that her official husbandmen hardly dared to call her own.

When England ceased to be part of Rome or, as her portentous Article states, "The Bishop of Rome hath no jurisdiction in this realm of England," she strove to remain Catholic. When she went into Schism, she tried to avoid Heresy, but the Puritans were too strong for her. The majority of the folk, and certainly the Bishops and Peerage, were willing to remain Catholics. Henry died Catholic in all but the Pope's Supremacy. This he parried by the joke of declaring his own Supremacy, which was as acceptable to the Churches of Europe as say the title of "Lord" George Sanger, the British Barnum, to the English Peerage. The

Church was left in England cut off like the Greek Church from Rome, but Doctrine and Orders might have stayed, had they not been pushed over the borderline under Edward VI into an Anglo-Catholicism, which Elizabeth accepted and which through many ups and downs remains the Church of England to this day. The Prayer Book over which the House of Commons went into fanatical debate in 1928 was the same volume which Cranmer cleverly composed to meet the crisis in 1550. An American schoolboy wrote that he translated the Old Testament into the New! He certainly turned the Old Missal into a new Prayer Book.

The Church of England rose out of its Prayer Book not out of the Bible, which it later gave to the folk in its most exquisite translation, that dedicated to King James and sometimes alluded to by American authors as the Version of St. James! Out of that version all the English-speaking sects have battened, but by the Prayer Book the Anglican Church will live or die. The Prayer Book was the Magna Charta of English compromise. It preferred what was deemed common sense to logic, piety to devotion, Parliament to Pope. It clung to the Apostles, but it cut the Apostolic See. Cranmer who had managed to be Primate under Henry and Edward, first under Schism and second under Heresy, unsuccessfully tried to recant and bob up orthodox under Mary. He was a master of facing both ways until he faced the flames. There were two Prayer Books under King Edward. The First in 1549 was the old Latin Liturgy in English and so Roman were the sources that Rome might almost have accepted it. The Sec-

ond Book in 1552 had Protestant amendments and the
famous Articles, referred to as "the forty stripes save one,"
were added later. They were intended to be Articles of
Peace enabling wild Protestants and tame Catholics to live
together under the old parish roof. Cranmer was the original type of Anglican Bishop, a cautious trimmer, veering
like a weather-vane, but a supreme scholar and in his
translations most marvelous. The English Litany remains
his masterpiece, though it no longer contains aspersions
upon the Pope or begs the prayers of Virgin, Angels, and
Patriarchs. The First Prayer Book opened to the New
Learning while the Second closed down on the Old. Cranmer thought more of orderly unction than of strict theology. Whatever his pen touched in the Latin services
flowered graciously until his English became as rife with
quotation as paragraphs of Shakespeare. His enemies have
said nothing well of him except that he burnt well. But
his Prayer Book has burned better and like a silver lamp
in the twilight still illumines every chancel in the whole
Anglican communion.

Let us see how his Book has fared in history. Its influence on English piety and prayer has been enormous.
If there were an Anglican Archangel, he would flutter its
leaves instead of a censer. On the National character it has
induced a love of compromise and substituted somnolency
for sanctity. English life became more and more a bed of
compromises. In the end Throne and Government, politics and religion have constantly become one thing while
meaning another. The Prayer Book is the great Compromise. Even the downright Harry was a compromiser. He

burnt Protestants while he executed Catholics. He sent England's merriest Chancellor to the block but fried the melancholy Genevan. He abolished Abbots but kept Bishops. He broke with the rock of Peter but he founded the See of Peterborough. He scattered Relics but he left the Mass untouched. The Second Prayer Book provided words of Consecration but left the power to consecrate in abeyance. This was the rub which the centuries have not rubbed away. Priests were retained as priestly as they wished to consider themselves, but Bishops could not ordain them in the manner of the Middle Ages. They were no longer to be sacrificing priests. They were intended to be something different and in that difference it was held that they lost the Apostolic Succession, which is the trademark under which Bishops hand their powers or gifts down the ages. Therein lay the great controversy whether Anglican Orders were valid or *in*-valid. So much of the old order had been kept, that it seemed a pity the Reformers crossed the line from Schism into Heresy, since Schism can keep the old Doctrine. This, of course, is the Roman view. The Anglicans themselves were always abundantly satisfied (with a few notable exceptions) that they had combined the best of two Churches and therefore deserved to enjoy the best of two worlds.

The English Prayer Book was gibberish to the Irish, the Welsh, and the Cornish, who called it "a Christmas game." The Irish rejected it in English and even more angrily when it was translated into Irish. The Welsh and Cornish remained in communion with the Pope as long as they had native Priests. They were afterwards netted by the forces of enthusiasm and dissent. But this is another story. It is sufficient that the English Prayer Book touched no Celtic fringe. Meantime Queen Elizabeth, though very much of a kitten, had perfectly observed the line of conduct between the serpent and the dove. Like Shakespeare she was a sceptic, who faced both religions and was unwilling to take risks for either. Witness her clever and equivocal lines on the Real Presence which Roman or Anglican could recite:

> "He was the Word that spake it.
> He took the Bread and brake it:
> And what the Word did make it
> I do believe and take it."

When she found the majority was Protestant, she decided that London was worth a Heresy, and suffered herself to be made Governess but not the Head of the Church. Rome had long been reproached with a Pope Joan, but Canterbury was now saddled with a *Papessa*. Her wisdom evolved the Elizabethan settlement. During the first few years of her reign open Protestants and secret Catholics were both deceived by the quiet cadence of the Prayer Book. The Articles were used as a rudder to steer away from Rome. It took the Council of Trent, the Jesuit Mission, and the Papal Bull against Elizabeth to awaken Roman Catholics to their position. Old Doctor Caius, a Cambridge Founder, for instance, remained a Roman Catholic in communion with the English Church until the coming of the Bull. Hence the historical importance of Jesuits like Campion and Parsons, who allowed no standing room betwixt Queen and Pope.

Queen Mary, whose unpopularity under the succeeding regencies gave the language its most popular word, had restored the old rite in Latin and perished within a few hours of her cousin and Primate Cardinal Pole. Her Bishops save one were deprived by Elizabeth, for they would not consecrate a Primate for her. Elizabeth favoured the old forms and, when she implanted a new Hierarchy, was angered if any married. The Commons were Protestant and ready for her lead. The old Peerage remained Catholic like the Episcopate and took generations to be eaten out by fines, marriages, and lawyers. The new Peerage was built out of the ruins of the Monasteries. The old West country rhyme sang now:

"Portman and Wyndham, Horner and Thynne:
When the Abbot went out, they came in."

The House of Cavendish arose from Wolsey's faithful Secretary. The House of Russell took the place of the Abbot of Woburn, and a thousand Priories and Friaries became sporting residences for the new gentry. Spelman's thrilling but unpopular *History of Sacrilege* contributed to the fairy tales of the Church. Nevertheless it was strange, as Spelman pointed out, how seldom new owners thrived with Church lands. The monk's curse became part of English romance and the modern ghost story dates from this period.

Elizabeth's decisive act was consecrating Archbishop Parker Primate. When she preferred her brother's Prayer Book to her sister's Missal, the Marian Bishops stayed with the Missal. Bishop Tunstall refused to consecrate Parker and she ordered Bishop Barlow to do so with the assist-

ance of Bishops Hodgkins, Scory, and Coverdale. Hodgkins was a true Bishop, but doubt was thrown on Barlow,
and as Anglican Orders descend through him, a controversy of terrific proportion evolved, to be hushed by the
Bull of Leo XIII declaring them null and void. A reading
of this Bull, *Apostolicae Curae,* and of the interesting
reply by the Anglican Archbishops, will save the trouble
of reading a library. To the antiquarian side may be added Mgr. Barnes' subsequent book on Barlow, pointing out
the strange fact that important Records are missing in
every See that Barlow occupied. In the Cathedral of Wells
there is a corbel representing a Bishop with children. This
was regarded as prophetic of Barlow's coming to that See.

Whether Barlow was a Bishop, or no Bishop, no one
dreamed of his historical importance at the time, or the
documents of his Consecration would not now be missing.
However, he consecrated Parker, though that was disbelieved by Catholics for fifty years until that unlucky
sportsman, Archbishop Abbot, showed the Lambeth Register to some Catholic Priests in prison. The assistant-Bish-
ops may have said the words with the full intention of
making a Bishop, but the expert Cardinal Pitra saw the
Register itself in 1852 and thought it apocryphal. Barlow
hardly realised his own importance, though by his five
daughters he became father-in-law to five Elizabethan
Bishops. Fuller gives Mrs. Barlow's Epitaph:

"So long she lived, so well her children sped,
    She saw five Bishops her five Daughters wed."

It seems common sense to admit that Parker and Barlow's sons-in-law became Bishops in an Anglican sense,

just as Mr. Pickwick might have consecrated his friends in a Pickwickian sense. Barlow may have been a Roman Bishop, but he cannot have intended to consecrate Parker one. But did he consecrate him in the sense of the Greek or Eastern Church? The controversy simmered until the Oxford Movement threw it on the crest of the wave.

The Church of England set out like a Catholic-fangled hulk, with a Protestant rudder in the hands of the State, under the strange mission to be neither Roman nor Greek, but a possible meeting place between East and West. She still floats like an Ark upon the floods of Dissent, which occupy the largest proportion of English-speaking Christianity. Whether she will find her Arrarat on the Roman rock or subside into the waters, history only can decide. But she remains the most interesting, the most important, and most historical Church outside the Roman Unity. The Oxford Movement proved a piercing test in many ways and an historian can only mark the results.

The spirit of Anglicanism has sucked wise compromise from the very cement of Church and State. A hundred further instances may be quoted of their composition, whether a King who may not exercise his Veto or Bishops who may not affirm a Dogma. And what judicious balancement decided that the Anglican could enjoy consecrated earth but not holy water? Bishop Montague under Charles I invoked Angels but not Saints. The dead were buried Eastward but Priests were officially forbidden to stand in the Eastward Position. The Protestants of the Establishment tolerated colour in windows but not in design upon the walls. The English soul was shocked by the

private use of the knotted Discipline but commended flog-
ging at Public Schools. The one was manly; the other,
sneaky. The Lord Mayor could come to Church arrayed
like Solomon in all his glory, but a Bishop in Cope and
Mitre might beware of brickbats. Though by her assumption of Bishoprics overseas she often seemed ridiculous,
her survival and increase in the Nineteenth Century is one
of the most remarkable religious facts in Christendom, to
be reckoned by historians with the birth of Wesleyanism.
Anglican Dioceses divided the world. Pope Gregory XVI
was amused to learn that Rome was in the Anglican Diocese of Gibraltar. But it was a later Pontiff, who when
asked to bless an Anglican Bishop, is said to have discreet-
ly murmured the Blessing reserved for incense before
burning!

But for the disputed defect in Orders, Anglicanism
could almost have made a parallel to Seventeenth Century
Gallicanism. In France and England the national Catholic
Church was reduced under the Civil Power. The English
were not less ready than the French to have ancient ceremonies performed with a decent moderation, but France
was jealous of the Papal Power and England shied at it.
The spirit of French Court Bishops was decidedly Anglican. Bossuet signing the Gallican Articles might well-
nigh have suited Canterbury as perfectly as his eloquence
would have adorned St. Paul's. From the Thirteenth Century, both the French and the English Kings have been
at war with the Pontiffs in the matter of Bulls and the decisions of Roman Congregations. With the post-Reforma-
tion opposition to the Pope in politics and Church affairs,

began the absolutistic age, and both Anglican and Gallican adopted the Divine Right of Kings. Jansenists, insisting on personal conversion and predestination, were the Puritans of the Gallican Church and during the long-drawn-out struggle, owing to the confusion injected by them, secured a temporary footing by the Peace of Clement IX, before their ultimate condemnation. Even certain among the French Jesuits, who were Ultramontane in theology, were Gallican in politics.

There was no part of the Gallican belief not to be found in some Anglican. Lord Acton recalled "Bramhall holding out a hand to Gallicans, Leighton consorting with Jansenists." Newman wrote of "the Creed which upholds Tradition with Laud, Consent of the Fathers with Beveridge, a Visible Church with Bramhall, Penance with Taylor, Prayers for the Dead with Ussher, Celibacy with Bingham." A modern Bishop's wife said her husband believed in the whole Catholic Creed except celibacy of the clergy! But for the defect in Orders, Anglicans and Gallicans might have figured together at the Vatican Council.

Anglicanism means Churches built by Wren, devotions composed by Andrewes, the poetry of Donne and Crashaw, the superb organ prose of Barrow. Under many diversifications Anglicanism preserves a unity of atmosphere though not of purpose.

Faber once summarised her phases deliciously as "the attempt to create a moderate party, doctrinally Roman, politically Anglican, by James and perhaps Charles (Archbishop Abbot strange to say favoured it: Laud broke it) so as to supply a middle term. Then a true Anglican

School among the Bishops and fostered by the Crown, trained in suffering, having three martyrs: a King, a Primate and a lay lord. Then the Nonjurors, thwarting the State and before strong enough to do so successfully, crushed. Then a gentle Georgian shelving down into a well-written, able, moral, gentlemanly Deism."

The Anglican savour runs rich in George Herbert's sacred but pliant poetry, in Isaac Walton's placid *Lives,* and the harmonious strength of Hooker, called the Judicious; in the fragrant power of Jeremy Taylor; above all in the Translation of the Bible ripe with all the richness of Tudor English. The English Bishops produced a book which like Fitzgerald's *Rubaiyat* may often be superior literature to its Oriental original.

The Prayer Book became the Anglican scrap book. The Oxford Movement found it full of fossils: Services for the landing of William of Orange and the pyrotechnics of Guy Fawkes Day; for Charles II in the Boscobel Oak and Charles I on the scaffold. Some of the Gospels on these festivals were *ben trovato:* for instance the Ninth Chapter of Luke for Guy Fawkes Day conveying Christ's answer to the request "wilt Thou that we command fire to come down from Heaven to consume them?" and for King Charles' Martyrdom the Twenty-First of Matthew, the parable of the husbandmen who killed the servants of the Lord of the Vineyard. The end of the Great Puritan Rebellion was commemorated on May 25; while on November 5 the beginning of another was no less cheerfully greeted and God thanked "for giving his late Majesty King William a safe arrival," as though Providence had preserved him from sea-sickness. With the course of the Oxford Movement these absurdities were slowly eliminated.

But the old Catholic liturgy, like a dead letter written in invisible ink, reappeared under application of warmth. The Communion Service was a shadowy Mass. The Psalms kept Latin headlines in memory of the old monastic chant. Matins were retained from the old Office Book and Evensong bespoke mediæval Vespers, though *Efansang* was the Tenth Century term. Calendar (apart from the Houses of Stuart and Hanover) kept the Apostles with the discreeter Feasts of Our Lady, who was needed to mark Quarter Day. The Annunciation was still kept on March 25; the date on which mediæval England began the year. This old New Year's day imposed by Henry II under Cistercian influence lasted until the reign of George II. The "Invention of the Holy Cross" remained to puzzle children, while antiquaries solemnly contended that St. Helena had been born at York. The choice of Saints was very select. St. George, St. Andrew and St. David were allowed to represent their countries, but the "united Church of England and Ireland" excluded St. Patrick. Kings like Edmund and Edward the Confessor remained, though the word meant little to Protestant schoolboys who sometimes wrote "Confectioner!" Both the Augustines stayed, as well as local ladies like Etheldreda and Margaret. St. Valentine, a priest in the Roman Calendar, is a Bishop for Anglicans, thanks to the Sarum rite. After the Reformation he took the place of Thomas of Canterbury in popularity and the Office of Venus with her ar-

rows and Cupids. St. Swithun, the first Saint to deal with
the English Climate, remained. Usages survived, which
the Roman has not retained. The English rule that Confirmation precedes First Communion dates to Archbishop Peckham in the Thirteenth Century. One marked
difference between Roman and Anglican is that the former counts Sundays after Pentecost and the latter after
Trinity. This was due to St. Thomas of Canterbury who
had introduced the Feast of the Trinity. His dead hand
may be indirectly traced upon the masterpieces of Cranmer and Chaucer.

The Anglican Ritual has been compared to a rubbish
heap but under the historical rubble lay broken jewelry
for the finding. Through the thin blood of the Establishment moved a memory from time to time of the pit out of
which she had been digged. She moved, but historians
could not say whether in the agony of a deathbed or like
a giant refreshed with sleep. Three times the Church of
England has moved out of slumber:

First: Under Archbishop Laud and the Caroline Divines.

Second: Under Archbishop Sancroft and the Nonjurors.

Third: Under John Henry Newman and the Tractarians.

The first and second adventures were prelude to the
third, which was the Oxford Movement proper. Like
three physicians, these three leaders tested their mother
church. Laud lost his head and Sancroft his Archbishopric
in the process, but both died in her arms. Newman alone
despaired of her and after making a piercing test passed
to Rome.

The main motive of the story is that the English people, save in Lancashire, had become deeply Protestant. The struggle with Spain had quickened a national religion and with the Jesuit Mission the Catholic remnant entered into the penal wilderness. Erastian and Puritan were constrained to use old Catholic buildings. There were always men of learning or enthusiasm, who insisted that only the Roman Jurisdiction had been cut and that the Catholic Order continued with the Creeds. Roman divines like Harding and Stapleton kept up a running protest, but in the end those who held with the Pope were hushed in the land.

The Papal cause had been involved with political fanatics as when Guy Fawkes essayed to blow up Parliament. Whatever history may conclude about Parsons, Campion was a delicious and fair controvert, the first to scatter Tracts in Oxford. Guy gave his name to the language and a new service to the Prayer Book called "Papists' Conspiracy," now discontinued. Like St. Catherine he remains a patron of fireworks.

Under King Charles I Archbishop Laud was inspired to ritualise the Church, ordering hats off in St. Paul's or erecting a Madonna over the porch of St. Mary at Oxford. Laud defined the theory that Rome, Constantinople, and Canterbury made a single three-branched candlestick. Charles II, while still an Anglican, sent a mission to Rome to ask for a Red Hat for d'Aubigny, his cousin. Constantinople was saluted and the Patriarch sent Charles I the Alexandrine Manuscripts of Scripture, which remain a national treasure. The Franciscan Sancta Clara, whom

Lord Acton placed as the greatest Catholic writer between Stapleton and Newman, tried to reconcile the Thirty-Nine Articles with Trent. Laud's Church policy was internal rather than foreign. He made the bitter mistake of persecuting Puritans. He enforced surplices and Sunday games. He upheld the Real Presence and like King Charles he died for the Church of England.

The reaction from Laud took the form of the Pilgrimship, the *Mayflower,* which is why the Bible and not the Prayer Book mystically unites Old with New England. The reaction from Charles resulted in the wreckage of all that remained beautiful or mediæval in English churches. Glass, imagery, screens, painting, and alabaster tombs were spoiled. Had Cromwell lived longer, the Anglican Episcopate would have become extinct. No Bishop was operative except Bishop Leslie of Raphoe, who was in arms. With Archbishop Bramhall of Armagh he kept up the ideal of Laud during the Commonwealth. Cromwell abhorred the Missal for religious and the Prayer Book for political reasons. The Prayer Book became the liturgy of the Stuarts and the scapegrace Charles II was added under a Restoration Service. The Gospel should have been the parable of the Prodigal Son, but the compilers added an Epistle from I Peter which the King must have smiled to hear. These were days of the Popish Plot and Charles only dared become a Catholic on his deathbed. The law only tolerated one Priest, Father Huddleston. He had saved the King's life in war and now, by a unique coincidence, may have saved his soul. James II succeeded in communion with Rome, but was constrained to exchange three King-

doms for an heavenly one. The Church of England fell
to the Whigs, though, while there was a Stuart Queen to
touch for the King's Evil, there was hope for the mystical. Queen Anne actually touched a boy who became Dr.
Johnson. Under Queen Anne, whose Bounty liveth
though her name is proverbially dead, Dr. Sacheverell
became the noisy martyr of the High Church. The
Church became immobile and isolated. Green, historian
and cleric, wrote "from that time to this the Episcopal
Church has been unable to meet the varying spiritual
needs of its adherents by any modifications of its government or worship." An effort was made to include Presbyterians at the Savoy Conference of 1662. Then all was still.
But there were stirrings as at Bethseda when an Angel
troubled the placid waters. Newman was the angel of the
Oxford Movement. Archbishop Sancroft and Bishop Ken
were the angels of the great renunciation known by the
name of Nonjurors.

The Nonjurors were the precursors of the High Church
and heralds of the Oxford Tractarians. Having taken the
Oath to King James they would not take the Oath to
King William. They would not box the compass or
change the captain of their ship. They were an abiding
protest against the Revolution of 1688. They were Jacobites in politics and something less romantic but more spiritual in religion. They gave up livings, benefices, and Bishoprics that their solemn word given to God might remain
unsundered by man. Their reward was poverty and suspicion in their lifetime and vile traduction by Macaulay
after death. Nothing was more distorted or graceless in his

History than his Old Bailey attack on the dead Nonjurors. They were the flies in the Whig ointment! Hallam felt equally uneasy and incurred the very epithets, scurrilous and intolerant, with which he reviled them. Bishop Burnet had naturally attacked them in his "romance or libel" describing his own *Times*. But they had smitten him and the time-servers. The books were loaded against the Nonjurors and Macaulay's schoolboys no doubt accepted his word that they had "sacrificed both liberty and order to a superstition as stupid and degrading as the Egyptian worship of cats." The Nonjurors are still widely forgotten. In modern times Nonjurors have been taken for a sect which declined to serve on Juries or have found a last use as the only English rhyme with Conjuror.

There were four hundred Nonjurors including the Primate and six Bishops. A majority of the clergy were with them but swallowed the Oaths, in many cases because they had nothing else to swallow. The Nonjurors preferred to starve on charity. They kept up a double fire of devotion and controversy. They avoided Rome but vomited the Whig Bishops, who intruded upon their Sees. When a chimney fell in a storm and crushed Bishop Kidder and his wife, the usurper of Ken at Wells, the Nonjurors saw the vengeance of Heaven. According to Macaulay: "Dr. Johnson pronounced that in the whole body of Nonjurors there was one and one only who could reason. The Nonjuror in whose favour Johnson made this exception was Charles Leslie." Leslie and Bishop Sheridan, the ancestor of the playwright, were the two Irish Nonjurors. Leslie denounced Archbishop King of Dublin for changing masters and King William for conniving at the Massacre of Glencoe. He withdrew into exile and tried to convert the Pretender to Anglican principles. His Tracts were an odd mixture of the rapier and the blunderbuss. L. M. Hawkins in *Allegiance in Church and State* has written: "The wide range of Leslie's vision and the depth of his insight enabled him to attain to an altogether bigger conception of the Church than that which found expression in the writings of the majority of his fellow Nonjurors. From his works there emerges an idea of the Catholic Church so vast and so profound that no claim which could be made on her behalf appears to demand too much."

The Nonjurors lost on the Divine Right of Kings but they won the great principle of freedom for the Church from the State Control, upon which the last battle of Anglicanism must be fought. Leslie in this regard laid down the lines afterwards followed by the Oxford Movement. He further wrote to Bossuet the view, which Rome obviously cannot accept, that "all particular Churches make up the whole which is the Catholic Church," and in his periodical the *Rehearsal* set forth the epigram, easily susceptible of misinterpretation, that "Kings are Bishops of the State and Bishops are princes of the Church." He believed that State and Church "can never clash on two parallel lines." He chose a *via media* between Presbyterian and Papal. Little hearkened him either Rome or the English laity! But the Oxford of Newman remembered many of his words long after his death.

The Nonjurors aimed at a Free State in a Free Church

and, when their deprived Bishops died, they continued a succession which only ended with Bishop Boothe in 1805. They clung to the Young Pretender, who graciously sent his child by Mrs. Walkinshaw to be baptized by Gordon the last Bishop of their regular body, for they had divided on Usages of Ritual such as the mixed Chalice and unleavened bread and the attitude to Rome. Leslie described one of them, Stevens, being refused by the Roman Chaplain at an Embassy: "Unless he would come up to their terms they would not go down to his. He told me with joy when a Grecian Archbishop was in England that he would try to be admitted by him but was refused there also." The nearest that the Churches of Rome and England came to reunion was during the time that Leslie was celebrating the Anglican Rite under the same roof at St. Germain beneath which the Pretender's Chaplain was saying Mass.

The Nonjurors being without money or books clung to the Universities till death. Wesley found Oxford "paved with the skulls of Jacobites." Catholics and Nonjurors lived precariously. They were bracketed by the Government in 1715 and the list made by Cosin was published with the values of their estates as a menace at the rebellion of 1745. The old Catholic names show what families clung to the old Faith: some to survive to this day and others to become extinct in blood or faith.

Until 1829, the year of Catholic Emancipation, George Eliot wrote that "rural Englishmen had hardly known more of Catholics than of the fossil mammoths." They were a curiosity not a menace. Their property in churches had been confiscated to the State, and of the thousands of buildings alienated at the Reformation few have been surreptitiously restored to Rome such as St. Etheldreda's, the Bishop of Ely's Chapel in London. There may be seen the Lion and Unicorn after solemn deposition. In a few Churches old Catholic families have asserted their right over the chancels in which their ancestors lie: The Duke of Norfolk at Arundel, the Tichbornes at Tichborne, and the Blunts at Maple Durham. The old Catholics were dying out fast. At the time of the Gordon Riots nine Peers left the Church and the faithful thought fit to rename themselves "protesting Catholic Dissenters."

What romance yet lies in the echo of the old Catholic names! Scroop of Danby, the holder of the Bend Or; Shirburne of Stonyhurst, where was planted the great College; Caryll of West Grinstead, and Fermor of Tusmore, recalling *the Rape of the Lock*. Eyre of Hassop kept Lord Derwentwater's shroud as their altar frontal. Fitzherbert of Norbury concealed a Royal marriage. With mingled feelings one peruses the list which reads now like a roll-call after battle:

  *Lord Arundell
   Lord Aston of Standon
  *Bedingfeld of Oxborough
   Biddulph of Biddulph
  *Blundell of Crosby
  *Blunt of Maple Durham
  *Bodenham of Rotherwas
   Brockholes of Claughton

*An asterisk marks those in the modern *Catholic Who's Who*.

Carey of Torr Abbey
Caryll of West Grinstead
*Lord Clifford
Clifton of Clifton
*Constable of Everingham
Curzon of Waterbury
*Lord Dormer
Errington of Beaufront
*Eyre of Hassop
*Eyston of East Hundred
Lord Fairfax of Gilling
Lord Fauconberg
Fermore of Tusmore
*Ferrers of Baddesley Clinton
*Fitzherbert of Norbury
Fleetwood of Gerard Bromley
Gage of Hengrave
Goring of Burton
*Haggerston of Haggerston
Herbert called Duke of Powis
Hesketh of Singleton
Hewett of Waresly
Holman of Workworth
*Howard of Corby
Huddleston of Sawston
*Jerningham of Cossey
Kemp of Slindon
Lewkenor of Eastbourne
Manby of Weale
Mannock of Stoke

Markham of Ollerton
Mollineux of Much Woolton
Lord Montague
Moore of Fawley
*Mostyn of Talacre
 Neville of Holt
*Lady Petre
 Plumpton of Plumpton
*Radcliffe of Capheaton
*Riddell of Swinburne
*Salvin of Croxdale
*Scroop of Danby
 Selby of York
 Sheldon of Weston
 Shirburne of Stonyhurst
 Simon of Ashton
 Southcott of Blyborough
*Earl of Stafford
 Stanley of Houghton
*Stonor of Stonor
 Tankred of Brampton
 Thimelly of Irnham
*Tichborne of Tichborne
 Timperley of Hinclesham
 Townley of Townley
*Vavasour of Haslewood
*Waterton of Walton Hall
 Webb of Great Canford
 Widdrington of Horsley

Such were the chief Catholic names published in 1745 when Prince Charlie went out for an earthly Kingdom. A wasting century passed until John Henry Newman set out for a spiritual one. Between the Reformation and the Oxford Movement the Church of England may be likened to a ladder, which Cranmer hoped the old Catholics would descend to meet continental Protestants halfway. Queen Mary made them briskly climb up to the top and Elizabeth brought them halfway down again. Laud started climbing and found himself climbing the scaffold. James II ordered them back to the top and lost ladder and all, while the Nonjurors were left hanging by their hands. The Whigs knocked the ladder to the ground and sat upon it, keeping matters in a very low and depressed state during the Eighteenth Century. The Bishops made the Church subservient to the new House of Hanover. "They chose to save the life of the Establishment by losing it." They handed over to Cæsar the very trinkets of the Sanctuary. There was little life and less grace. Grace went to the rising Methodists and life was stultified in the Bangorian Controversy. Hoadly, Bishop of Bangor, attacked the Nonjurors and the mystic Nonjuror, William Law, replied. The Nonjurors were overwhelmed by indifference not by reason. They became like the old Catholics, "a shrinking and ineffective communion," but resurrection awaited both. Law wrote the *Serious Call,* from which Wesley dated his revival. In 1733, exactly a hundred years before the Oxford Movement started, Whitefield met the Wesleys. Wesley himself was a High Churchman anxious about strict ritual until he suffered conversion and found-

ed one of the world Churches in his tracks. Then Methodists preached like the Friars before and the Salvationists
after them. Parson Crabbe described their effects in the
fields:

"Soft women fainted, prouder man expressed
Wonder and woe and butchers smote the breast."

Their reaction on the Church of England produced the
Evangelicals. The Oxford Movement arose from living
Evangelical and dead Nonjuror. The two strains met in
Newman.

The Evangelicals were reflected in Cowper's *Hymns,*
Young's *Night Thoughts,* and Venn's *Complete Duty of
Man,* which was a Calvinist's answer to the *Whole Duty*
thereof, which remains anonymous, but may have been
penned by Archbishop Frewen, who at Magdalen College set up the first altar since the Reformation.

Wesley remained in the Church of England, but his
teaching won the Cornish and the Welsh, who had retained the enthusiasm without the Sacraments of the old
Church. The Welsh still crossed themselves, blessed their
beds, and prayed for the dead. Wales was priestless because Welsh and English Catholics had quarrelled at
Rome. Wales was left to the Anglicans, who failed to hold
the Celtic people. A hundred years later every moun-
tain in Wales was a stronghold of Wesley and Dissent.
The loss of Wales was a tragedy which still calls for historical enquiry.

The English people were willing to be cut off from
Rome and hindered her agents, but the Welsh had desired
them in vain. It is interesting that Laud once planned

reunion with a Welsh Benedictine from Douay. In England Methodism like the Reformation and Puritanism swept the lower class. All Catholic revivals touched the aristocracy. Selina Lady Huntingdon, who became the nursing mother of Methodism, was an exception. It makes a link with history that she brought the old Duchess of Marlborough to hear Whitfield. The Church of England was not defended by mystical virtues or flaming champions, but by Test Acts which prevented Dissenters from sharing the loaves and fishes and by portentous Bishops, who kept the larger portion from their own clergy. The Bishops naturally disapproved of Enthusiasts and Evangelicals. They patronised the dullest of controversies: that between those, who believed in a little dogma, and those who believed in none. They left nothing behind them but comic and preposterous monuments worthier of the Museum than the Cathedral. The Church wallowed in a slough of domestic Simony. Younger sons held rich livings and worthy men were left to starve. Betwixt plutocrat Bishop and starveling Curate merrily hunted the "Squarsons," who as Squires and Parsons added a new Commandment which was reckoned the most important of all: "Thou shalt not poach thy neighbour's Land, neither his hare nor his pheasant nor any game that is his!"

II

THE FIRST PHASE

The Oxford Movement sprang like an exotic flower out of fallow and dust. The Movement itself was the tinted dawn of the Victorian Era and symbolised that coming period of strife. The realms of thought, philosophy and belief in England were still uncontested. Intellectual England resembled Africa before being rushed by the rival powers. The Victorians grew less settled and content in their souls. Their social and material fabric stood, as they thought, like the pyramids, but there was no field of creed or intellect over which champions and prophets did not conquer or perish in Homeric warfare. The struggle for Oxford between the new Movement and the old guard in possession resembled the war of Greeks and Trojans.

Before the dawn there fell an exquisite and multicoloured dew, the romance of Sir Walter Scott. The past not only of Scotland but of the mediæval rose gently from the dead. He loved monkish Latin and caught the scenery if not the soul of the Middle Ages. There were novels dedicated to the *Abbot* or the *Monastery* full of more or less inaccurate Catholicism. The Jesuit as well as the Covenanter passed guilelessly before the reader. The pomp, the beauty, the cruelty, the mystery, the strength associated in his mind with the old religion was flung by a sorcerer's pen into the stately homes of England. In quietly leisured and undistracted days the ink of Scott flowed like roseate lava over honest and enthusiastic souls. Scott no more dreamed that he was reviving Romanism in the Church than that he was persuading the War Office to restore chain armour. Scott moved not as a mitred priest but as a minstrel. He had recalled Crusader and monk and even a creaky old ritual. The thirst which he engendered for Romance led to desires for Rome. His Gothic toy of Abbotsbury signalled a revival in the Sacristy. Sir Walter sowed where Newman was to reap. With the *Stabat Mater* on his lips he died in 1832. In the next year came the Oxford Movement.

Eighteen thirty-two was also marked by the Reform Bill. It was the year which really ended the Eighteenth Century. Centuries do not properly close in double zeros. In English History the Seventeenth Century ended with the Revolution in 1688 and the Sixteenth in 1603 with the death of Elizabeth. The excitement leading to the Reform Bill had stirred the Church. The Bishop of Bristol had his Palace burnt and, sad to say, Archbishop Howley was mobbed in Canterbury. On November 5 the Guys burnt in Cathedral Cities suspiciously resembled Bishops. Government felt that something must be done and uncourageously suppressed ten Anglican Sees in Ireland. On July 14, 1833, this was denounced by Keble in a famous Sermon on National Apostacy, described as "a mixture of the sublime and the insignificant," preached in St. Mary's, Oxford. Thence Newman dated the birthday of the Move-

ment, of which he was to be the life and which in turn
was to prove his Anglican death. The Victorian Century,
which closed in 1914, had begun.

If the Church of England had been more freely visited
by flame, the sign might have been regarded as Pente-
costal. It needed firing badly for the supernatural was
dead or very dusty. The best Parsons were reflected in the
works of Goldsmith, Fielding, and Sterne. But the Vicar
of Wakefield was not, in Scott's words, the type "predes-
tined to be a glorified Saint!" They kept dull Diaries and
dined upon tithe pig. They enjoyed country life and cher-
ished such crumbs of sport and lees of wine as reached
them from the Squire's table. Some hunted and some merited benefices by marrying the cast mistress of a patron. A
fishing parson kept his live bait in the font.

The beautiful old churches were rich with the mouldy
deposit of the Middle Ages. They were stuffed with high
box pews, "whether to conceal disorder or to proclaim
pride." Squires sat round charcoal fires in their cushioned
seats, while servants and labourers from high galleries
prayed God bless King and Squire and Squire's relations.
Three-deckers combining pulpit and desk rose like wood-
en pagodas, from the lowest tier of which the Parish
Clerk supplanted the mediæval acolyte like a gargoyle.
Female pew-openers in town had to be tipped, while bea-
dles smote the poor or ushered the rich with heavy wands.
In London fashionable preachers buzzed under sounding-
boards in private Chapels. Hannah More and Wilberforce
toured thirteen Parishes in Gloucestershire ("as sure as
God's in Gloucestershire" was the mediæval proverb) to

report that the only discoverable Bible was used to prop a flower-pot. In the country there proceeded from lofts and galleries the sound of fiddles and barrel-organs and all manner of wheezy music. People sat or knelt "balancing between the chest and the end of the back." Gentlemen prayed as though consulting Urim and Thummin, in their top hats.

Doctrine was nowhere. Sacraments, except for formalities, had gone with the Nonjurors. Baptisms were performed in a mass. Cases were known where even water was dispensed with. At Confirmation sponsors were collected on the street for the price of a pint of beer. The wife of a West Country Bishop gave Confirmation Balls. A broad-minded Bishop described Confirmation as "a perfectly unobjectionable Ceremony." Communion was little more than taking wine with the Parson, who handed what remained to the Sexton to drink. When the Manchester Churchwardens complained that weekly Communion was a burden on the rates, the Bishop of Chester politely made it a quarterly proceeding. The Bishops, whose names were as often written in the Peerage as in the Book of Life, were wonderful to record. Shute Barrington of Durham took his foxhounds on visitation. Watson of Llandaff passed a studious life away from his See. He built an elegant Palace on Windermere which unluckily was not in his Diocese. At his Cambridge residence he strengthened an upper room for parties, which proved useful a century later when used for Mass by the Catholic Chaplain to the University. The chief Bishop whose name survives is Malthus, who wrote his famous Essay on Population, whether he was troubled by agricultural distress or the fecundity of Parsons.

The English Bishops were as disgraceful as many of the French before the Revolution. At the dawn of the Oxford Movement a new type had arisen called "Greek Play Bishops." To have edited a Latin Missal would have been a less qualification. As Disraeli said, Peel sought "successors of the Apostles among third-rate hunters of syllables."

Yet there was no conscious irreverence. The Church was always in the hands of gentlemen. Kegan Paul recalled a Vicar turning to the Communicants with: "Has any lady or gentleman a Corkscrew?" like a Conjuror addressing his audience. At Eton in the Eighteenth Century members of the Sixth Form received Communion once a term or were fined a guinea. Holy Tables, when worn out, were sent to the taproom. Chalices decorated the tables of the rich. A famous racehorse was called Crucifix. Ash Wednesday was so moveable a feast that at Lichfield one year it was postponed a week to suit the Fair of the name. The hunting parsons were a civilised throw-back to the fighting Bishops of the Middle Ages. The unwritten code allowed them to hunt but not to race. Pugin recorded that "in Lincoln the son of the late Bishop, who refused to subscribe to the erection of his throne, lost £7,000 at the last Lincoln Races." And J. E. C. Bodley told how Archbishop Harcourt contrived to drive past the York Races in coach and six. The upper Clergy were men of the world, but good men of the world. They thought it ungentlemanly to interfere with private life. They only asked for the cloak of respectability against Jacobin and Dis-

senter. The Jacobin, not the Jacobite, was their real enemy and critic. Benbow's *Crimes of the Clergy* appeared
in 1823 and was suppressed. It was a fearful but sometimes
amusing Calendar. Crimes of turpitude can be thrown at
the black sheep of any Church and are unworthy of cita-
tion, but there was something very English in Mr. Wright
of Boughton who was accused of singing the Athanasian
Creed to a fox-hunting tune! He was preferable to the
Clergyman who once apologised for mentioning Christ
in a Christmas Sermon!

At the Universities the standards were low. The Articles
of Religion were signed with punctilious indifference. At
Cambridge the celibate Fellows were accorded unhal-
lowed connections. But Simeon of King's for fifty years
had preached and revived religion. A century has passed
and the landing halfway to his rooms is still called the
Saint's Rest. To this day the Oxford Movement is coun-
tered by Simeon's Trustees who purchase Benefices in a
manner that makes Simeony akin to Simony. Oxford har-
boured neither piety nor learning. Lord Chesterfield said
that Oxford would only be known to exist owing to the
treasonable spirit avowed there. Treason to State had melt-
ed. Treason to the established Church was yet to come.
The Church at best was philanthropic and only wished
her children not to conspire or inspire. She was not dis-
satisfied since she had no competition. Church and State
cohabited in an atmosphere of great security. The Church
cringed and the State patronised. They never conflicted
and civil Divorce was hardly known. It required an Act
of Parliament to break wedlock. Anglican principles had

apparently attracted the favour of God and the Empire of the world. To those recalling the fate of Louis XIV, Philip of Spain, and Napoleon it seemed as though Heaven favoured the Book of Common Prayer. Revolution was coming, but in the most unexpected and subtle manner: a Catholic revival in the National Church.

Let us link history. The victor of Waterloo had made a pale and ascetic Student of Christchurch, Professor of Hebrew at Oxford. His name was Edward Bouverie Pusey, of a family so old that they held the manor of Pusey by a horn from Canute. Pusey was an old Etonian and had studied theology in Germany. He became the Anglican anti-Pope. Here are two measurements: Dean Hutton described him as "surpassingly sincere, profoundly erudite, piercingly appellant": Cardinal Manning, as "intellectually contrary, suicidal, ecclesiastically unlawful, foolish."

Meantime a band of choice spirits collected at Oriel College under Provost Hawkins: Whately, the Wilberforce brothers, Keble, Newman. They conversed in a hushed agitation and as a grim innovation the teapot was served instead of College Port. They peered abroad and desired better things. Whately taught Newman Logic and passed on, the first to see and fear the ghost of Mysticism. Newman made a nervous trip in the Mediterranean and on an Orange boat wrote the *Pillar of Cloud* from which the world has since drawn Kindly Light. He felt a task before him which became clearer after Keble's clarion sermon. In September he began to issue *Tracts for the Times.* Oxford was unready for Times or Tracts. Nobody of age or position visioned the dynamic powers flickering in the young men.

Not by Tract alone did Newman work but by every word which proceeded out of his mouth as Vicar of St. Mary's. The delivery of those sermons in the dim light of the University Church has been often described. Even his bitterly critical brother wrote how "the perfume of spirituality with literary beauty and original thought settled like dew from Heaven on some older Oxonians." And around Oriel rose the men whose creed was Newman. The Church was described as "the Newmanitish Phantasm," but the Tractarians were no men of straw. As Dean Church, the historian of the Movement, said: "For their time and opportunities the men of the Movement with all their imperfect equipment and their mistakes still seem the salt of their generation." In their enthusiasm they carried the Tracts by coach and saddle, leaving them on bewildered parsons. Whatever Newman touched in the marbled and mouldy cemetery of Anglicanism seemed to flower. The principles of the Nonjurors moved in the dust. The martyrdom of Laud seemed to sanctify Oxford. To the old English Divines the Tractarian made solemn conjuration and appeal: to Ken and Beveridge; to Bull, who had been thanked by the Gallican Church for his defence of the Nicene Creed; to Butler and Lancelot Andrewes, who had told Cardinal Bellarmine he believed as much as he in the Real Presence. In the same year a young man entered English politics as the hope of the unbending Tories; Mr. Gladstone, who became Newman's most distinguished follower.

Newman was far from carrying Oxford. It was only the young men who rallied to him. The Heads and Tutors were strongly averse with few exceptions such as Ward of Balliol. Whately and Arnold, who had influenced him, became suspicious and hostile. Both were Erastian and believed in the State above the Church. Ironical one and enthusiastic the other, they were given appropriate spheres: Arnold to civilise the Public School and Whately an Archbishopric in John Bull's other Parish.

But the flower of Oxford walked with Newman and no Dons could prevent eager youth hearing his sermons. Amongst his disciples were the Froudes, sons of an Archdeacon famous for horse-jumping; Hurrell and James, but Newman lost them both. Hurrell died young leaving his glittering *Remains,* which showed a boyish ascetic delighting in parry and paradox: hating the Reformers and loving the Nonjurors. He was the herald of the new Movement, laughing and often seeing clearest ahead. He was tolerant to the Papacy and wished to call the new party Apostolical. After probing his own soul and trying the spirits of others in more ways than one, he passed over and none could say whether he would have followed or preceded Newman to Rome. He must have stirred a forgiving smile in the countenance of the Tractarians when he called Law's *Serious Call* a "clever book." As Keble said: Why not call the Day of Judgment a pretty sight? When they grew older and climbed into historical niches they remembered and mourned one who had been the symbol of their spiritual youth.

His brother James walked awhile with Newman, like Mark Pattison, and then both turned aside, Pattison to be Rector of Lincoln and Froude to write his *Nemesis of*

Faith, which pained the Liberals and scandalised Tories, but carried fine pictures of Newman and of Carlyle, who from outside looked upon the Movement as a Miasma and wrote of "spectral Puseyisms." Nevertheless Carlyle's character, the Abbot Samson, carved out of the annals of St. Edmundsbury Abbey, achieved more than all the Tracts in reconciling the English people to what had once been. Froude's life was a tour in search of a hero in life and of the picturesque in language. For a time he found both in Newman. He helped him with his *Lives of the Saints,* finishing one on St. Neot's with a sceptical flourish. He made a virtue of inaccuracy. In later days he wrote without a vestige of authority: "St. Patrick I found once lighted a fire with icicles, turned a French marauder into a wolf and floated to Ireland on an altar stone!" As the Irish Bishop said of *Gulliver's Travels,* it was stuffed with lies!

In his *Short Studies* Froude wrote an embittered criticism of the Movement. He held that the English Church was healthy and happy before it was distracted by Oxford Thought and Romanised by Anglo-Catholic pretence. It was a national growth "and as you do not ask of a tree if it is true but is it alive, so with an Established Church." The land he believed full of such rare beings as the clergyman depicted in Wordsworth's *Excursion.* Controversy slept and scepticism was only a harmless speculation. People went to Church because Christianity was in their fibres. The Anglican system from Beadle to Archbishop of Canterbury seemed part of the existing order of the Universe. It did not occur to any that such a satisfactory arrangement could come to an end or should be changed.

JOHN HENRY CARDINAL NEWMAN
(From an old engraving)

Then came Newman, and good clergymen became "pilot-fish for the Roman missionaries." The change in outlook Froude described deliciously as well as succinctly: "History was reconstructed for us. I had learnt like other children that the Pope was Antichrist and that Gregory VII had been a special revelation of that being. I was now taught that Gregory VII was a saint. I had been told to honour the Reformers. The Reformation became the Great Schism, Cranmer a traitor and Latimer a vulgar ranter. Milton was a name of horror and Charles I was canonised. Similarly we were to admire the Nonjurors, to speak of James III instead of the Pretender and to look for Antichrist not in the Pope but in Whigs."

Keble's *Christian Year* preceded the Tracts by five years like a Greek Chorus full of melodious and mystic prelude of what was to come in sterner fact. The *Christian Year* reads now like the feeble piping of Pan caught and confirmed in a rural rectory. Keble wrote like Wordsworth, in a surplice, and according to Pusey that Laureate wished to assist a revision. It seemed good in comparison with his own *Ecclesiastical Sonnets* which covered the history of Anglicanism, sometimes to the harpstring but too often to the beat of bathos. Keble was tame and misty but he secured the overwhelming admiration of Churchmen who admired his verse as the bride admires her own wedding cake. Being a true poet he could not fail to touch grandeur and he wrote, in Professor Saintbury's opinion, three grand poems:

"What went ye out to see" (Third Sunday in Advent),

"See Lucifer like lightning fall" (Third Sunday in Lent),

"O for a sculptor's hand" (Second Sunday after Easter).

Whately called Keble a "caged eagle" and his finest poetry resembled the moultings of such. Keble was not hindered by the agonies of indecision and change and attained his highest possible. Whether Newman could have been a great poet cannot be known. Only in times of langour and stress could poetry break from him. A gulf of interval lies between *Lead Kindly Light* and the *Dream of Gerontius*. Faber could certainly have been a great poet, and Wordsworth sadly confessed that in him England had lost a laureate. No poet has attained the shuddering contemplation of his *Sorrowful World*. Faber's *Eternal Years,* which comforted Newman himself, is the rhythm of a Marcus Aurelius turned Carthusian. Newman described them as the words of one who had found, compared to one seeking the quest of *Lead Kindly Light*. Faber's gift passed into impassioned sermons. It remains to be said that the finest religious lyric of the Movement, *The Burial of Moses,* was written by the wife of Archbishop Alexander, who had followed Newman a while.

The *Christian Year* was the Psalter of the Tractarians. It is now unread as poetry and unsung as Hymns. The Third Edition had six additional poems, including one for Guy Fawkes day, "an address to Converts from Popery" with the cautious lines:

"O come to our Communion Feast:
There present in the heart,
Not in the hands, the Eternal Priest
Will His true self impart."

From his deathbed Keble changed the negative as

though to accord with the advance in doctrine of the English Church.

Precursors there were of Newman, like Kenelm Digby who became a Catholic in 1825. Without any style or proportion in his writings he collected the mediæval scrapbooks called the *Broadstone of Honour* and *Mores Catholici*. He wrote in the prodigal and prodigious manner of the *Anatomy of Melancholy*. He could not bear a fragment to be lost. He wrote as though Quixote had become a scholar instead of a Knight. For him modern life was like "the wind through a ruined cell" and Catholicism could not be political or commercial. By him "Young England" was inspired and Disraeli and Ruskin learnt chivalry in Economics.

The Catholic Revival in England seemed to exemplify the saying that Catholicism was the religion of the gentlemen of Europe. The Middle Class stayed Protestant and the only Catholic labourers in England were a growing flood from Ireland. Other precursors were Sibthorpe of the old Yorkshire name who became priest, parson, and priest again. From Cornwall old Sir Harry Trelawney was ordained and it was hinted that a more than natural power of retentive memory was vouchsafed, when he said his First Mass at the English College in Rome where Father Ignatius, Lord Spencer's son, soon afterwards preached his first sermon. The Tractarians regarded them as deserters.

The Tractarians found that their real enemy was not the deaf Evangelical nor the blind Protestant but the State. Statesmen, with the exception of the rising Gladstone, were Erastian, a word which lies at the root of the whole Anglo-Catholic struggle. The State claimed to lay down doctrine and ritual on the ground that whoever paid the piper picked the tune. Charles Leslie had written that the Erastian idea made the gentry Deists and the people Dissenters. No wonder the Tractarians clung to the Nonjurors, who made the money sacrifice rather than obey the State. "The arguments of the Nonjurors burst into new life in the Tractarian agitation" (Hawkins in *Allegiance in Church and State*.) The *Tracts for the Times* were a restatement of the Nonjurors in modern terms. Leslie's *Regale and Pontificale* was republished in 1838 as "an antidote to the opinions which still prevail" and both Gladstone and Manning declared they held by it. Lathbury's *History of the Nonjurors* appeared in 1845 in answer to Bishop Blomfield's scornful remark that Apostolical Succession had gone with them. This Blomfield was Bishop of London when the Oxford Movement broke out. He objected to the cult of Martyrs as "deified sinners," and made other statements sore to the Oxford men. He stated as a matter of mild pride, in 1834, that he had only sixty-four Parishes without a resident clergyman. Unkind critics revealed that he had been a non-resident himself of a Cambridge Parish, whose weekly account was forwarded to him by the Curate in a vegetable basket! In 1807 less than 5,000 out of 11,000 Parishes in England had resident clergy. During the preceding score of years, under Bishop Porteous, not one new church was built in London. Since the Oxford Movement one quarter of the Anglican churches have been built. Blomfield once ordered the surplice in the pulpit and then withdrew before the storm. The surplice which had brought a Scotch army against King Charles provoked riot long into the days of Queen Victoria.

Spelman's *History of Sacrilege* was brought up to date by J. M. Neale with a formidable list of crimes and disasters attending the possessors of Abbey lands. Even the misfortunes of Walter Scott and Byron were attributed to possession of Abbotsbury or Newstead Abbey. Neale sang "the Curse of the Abbeys" in a spirited Hymn, which as yet has not been included in any Church use:

"Ill hands are on the Abbey Church
 They batter down the Nave:
They strip the lead, they spoil the dead,
 They violate the grave . . .
Thou dravest forth the monks at large
 And mad'st their wail thy mock.
Ho! Thomas Baron Cromwell
 Prepare thee for the block!
Lord Falkland, thy ancestral crimes
 Must fall upon thy head.
St. Alban's curse at Newbury
 Prepares thy bloody bed.
Lord Stafford, innocent in vain,
 The snare is round thee set!
Lord Russell, stoop thee to the axe
 For Woburn claims her debt."

Dusty and unread the Tracts lie in many a Library. It was upon them that the new revival of religious life through England has been laid. Like the rubble buried at great foundations out of sight and almost of remembrance are the Oxford Tracts. Is there anyone living who has read them in their entirety? Yet once they inspired two Universities and shook the National Church.

They seem exceedingly dull and Newman was amused hearing that a great scholar used them to rest his mind from the excitement of the Greek Subjunctive. Newman commenced with a burst of irony, suggesting Martyrdom as "a blessed termination" for English Bishops and adding: "we touch not their sword and crosier. Yet surely we may be their shield-bearers without offence." When crosiers eventually came into play it was upon the poor shield-bearers that they rapped heaviest. Other shafts of Newmanic irony were the suggestion that Angels came and sat in the empty pews of the Establishment, or the line in the *Lyra Apostolica* presumably referring to Anglican Bishops:

"In dew and cold the anointed warriors sleep."

Newman and Keble led off the Tracts. Hurrell Froude wrote No. 9, a comforting suggestion on shortening Church Services. Had he lived, he might have disclaimed High and Broad in favour of Short Church. In 15 and 19 Newman and Palmer introduced the Apostolic Succession. Perceval, a Court Chaplain, wrote No. 36 on the English Sects, which he divided into those who teach too much or too little of the Truth. Amongst those who erred on the side of excess he counted Swedenborgians, Southcotians and Romanists. Newman's *Via Media* appeared in 38 and 41. Other Tracts reprinted writings of Nonjurors and Caroline Divines. Of the literal Tractarians who wrote the Tracts only Newman and Manning reached Rome. The Tracts were anti-Roman.

Tract 18, on Fasting, Pusey initialed, whereat the angry Evangelicals fell upon the hapless name, for Newman's was kept anonymous. Henceforth "Puseyite" was a stick or a standard or a stumblingblock to the distracted Church until the Bishop of Worcester forbade the word in Church. But the Pope, Gregory XVI, had begun to talk about *Puseyista,* though his successor failed of pronunciation and used to ask devout converts for news of Pussy! From the Roman watch tower Dr. Wiseman was soon busy and Newman made Tract 71 a counter-shield to the Roman thrust. Tract 78 is not generally known to have been the joint work of Manning and Marriott.

There was no alarm while Newman appeared only to be lifting his influence, in the words of Froude, against "Bentham politics and Paley religion, prebendal stalls and pony-gigging parsons." Church and State could hardly fear dissolution at the hest of that strange apparition stealing through the Oxford Streets in blacktail coat, his lustrous eyes harnessed to goggles but illuminating his pallid face.

With Tract 90, however, "Remarks on certain passages in the 39 Articles," Newman invoked the storm, and there was no Tract 91. The Tracts had spread like wildfire through a dry Church, but as Dean Church wrote: "it was not till Newman made up his mind to force on the public mind in a way which could not be evaded the great Article of the Creed, I believe in One Catholic and Apostolic Church, that the Movement began."

Tract 90 was the most famous Tract in Church history. It symbolised the Anglican past and indicated a future. A parable will cover the ground. The Articles in the Prayer Book were like a red tail added to a blue kite, if we may take red for Protestant and blue for Catholic. The compilers of the Prayer Book had hoped for a purplish effect. But then as ever the red and blue elements waged war. Under Laud the blue element went top. The Nonjurors were bluish, but the Whigs reddened them out. The Church remained a sombre red during the Eighteenth Century. The Tractarians restored the blue and Newman carrying war into red territory wrote Tract 90 to prove that, though the Articles were written in red, they were written on blue paper!

He insisted they were anti-Roman but not anti-Catholic. They condemned the abuses not the uses of Purgatory and the Mass. The most he would allow Rome was that "she alone amid all the errors and evils of her practical system has given free scope to the feelings of awe, mystery, tenderness, reverence, devotedness and other feelings which may be especially called Catholic."

He concluded his Tract by saying: "the Protestant Confession was drawn up with the purpose of including Catholics, and Catholics will now not be excluded. What was an economy in the Reformers is a protection to us. What would have been a perplexity to us then is a perplexity to Protestants now. We could not then have found fault with their words: they cannot now repudiate our meaning."

The meaning given by Newman was quickly repudiated. Dean Close said he would be sorry to trust the author of Tract 90 with his purse. It was the end of the Tracts. It was the beginning of the end for Newman as an Anglican and had it not been for a new outburst of stubborn, almost blind strength, it would have been the end of the Church of England. Newman wrote a letter to the *Times* signed "Live and let live," but it was refused publication.

For the next five years Oxford was a cock-pit. Newman made no appeal to Cambridge or ever preached there, but in an early poem he wrote of those using Private Judgment as "all wranglers and all wrong," which Cambridge men have considered a slight on themselves. Cambridge, though the home of muscular Christianity and the mother of Charles Kingsley and Simeon, reacted as she always does to her sister. The young men scrambled equally for a Part of Pickwick or a Tract from Oxford. It is doubtful if at the beginning of the century there was a single Roman Catholic in Cambridge. The future Cardinal Acton was at Magdalene in the 'Twenties, though he had to ride thirty miles to hear Mass. Cambridge was as well-plenished as Oxford with mediæval buildings and woke quietly to her sister's call. Great contrasts always lay between the Universities. Bitterly it was once said that Cambridge had produced Protestant Martyrs and Oxford burnt them. Dean Stanley said that Oxford produced great Movements and Cambridge great men. In the Caroline revival all the great men except Laud were Cantabs. But the great men of the Oxford Movement were all Oxonians. It was true that Oxford adopted lost causes while Cambridge preferred discovering them. If Oxford was dreaming of a lost Catholicism, Cambridge gave her practical aid. The Cambridge Camden Society was founded to investigate and restore old churches. The Camdenites gradually changed the face of public worship. Oxford produced the Thought and Letterpress of the Movement, but Cambridge men made the illustrations. At Cambridge arose the greatest of liturgiologists, Henry Bradshaw, to whose memory a Society of his name continues to issue rare liturgical material. Hugh Rose, in whose Suffolk Rectory, the first Tractarians met, was a Cambridge man.

Greatest of the Camdenites was J. M. Neale, who gave his Church her greatest Sisterhood and translated the Latin Hymns in versions that have been used by Anglican and Roman ever since. He gave England *Good King Wenceslaus, Jerusalem the Golden,* and a score of the hymns which are mouthed wherever the British flag flies. Another Cantab, Beresford Hope, played with the "Young England" Movement, which was Disraeli's young dream of giving the Church to the People with sprigs of nobility in the leadership. Hope built churches and founded the *Saturday Review* as the High Church oriflamme.

The Camden Society unearthed Jocelyn of Brakelond out of which Carlyle wove his vista of a mediæval Abbot. The local Church of the Holy Sepulchre was restored and provided with a stone altar whereat a Judgment was given against stone altars in the Church of England. The Camden men arose in a land where the clergy contentedly "gave cautious sermons in bleak churches." They were not content to play at "innocent antiquarians." They rode out in squadrons to investigate and restore broken-down churches; a pious form of "steeple-chasing." Beresford Hope and

Benjamin Webb poured forth Catholic art and liturgy in the *Ecclesiologist* to a bewildered England. Ecclesiology covered a good deal of doctrine without alarming patrons. As Hope wrote: "the Oxford Movement is essentially controversial but (the Cambridge) ecclesiologists talk quietly of other Churches and other rites as if no breach had occurred." Hope restored the Abbey of St. Augustine at Canterbury, the seed ground of English Christianity having descended to a pothouse and billiard room. He planned with the American Bishop of Wisconsin to divert Finnish emigrants from Lutheran to Anglican error. He was not a Ritualist, being described as "a Hook and Hooker type of Churchman." He was the Gladstonian type of Churchman. He carried independence into public life, voting for Church against Party and calling Disraeli "an Asian mystery" in the House. Webb and Neale published a translation of Durandus and Symbolism became known to the Church of England. Before long Romanising wolves were suspected to be wearing the wool of Gothic sheep. The great Gallican Montalembert had been elected a Member of the Camden Society. The Bishop of Down resigned and issued a violent attack. Dr. Close preached "to show that as Romanism is taught analytically at Oxford, it is taught artistically at Cambridge." The Camden Society was dissolved, but as Kenneth Clark writes in *The Gothic Revival,* "Through them more than any other agency the Tractarians gained their ultimate victory. For fifty years almost every new Anglican church was built according to their instructions."

Few Cambridge men moved towards Rome. Neale confessed that "when we discovered the Reformers to be villains and the Articles trash we had some thoughts of Rome." But he took refuge in his love for the Greek Church, actually rejecting the *Filioque* clause from the Creed of the West. "Depend upon it the Greeks are right," he wrote. As a University, Cambridge struggled officially against the Oxford Movement. Her Colleges and Churches remained profoundly low with two or three exceptions. Her inspiration stayed Evangelical after the pattern of Simeon and Henry Martyn. She preferred to send Low Church missionaries abroad rather than High Church apostles to the home dioceses. The Camden men departed with their dreams of which one was interesting. Neale planned "to erect in Cambridge a large church called St. Alban the Protomartyr. The style to be decorated with lofty cathedral spire." Fifty years later this vision was literally fulfilled in the church dedicated to the English Catholic Martyrs, but under Papal auspices.

From Cambridge came the finest estimate of the Oxford Movement and its leader. In his *History of English Patriotism,* Mr. Wingfield Stratford describes how:

"The figure of the glowing and saintly Newman towers like a colossus above the Whewells and Kingsleys and Jowetts, above the Arnolds and Mills and Spencers of the Victorian age. He seemed in his mournful grandeur a being superior to the frailties and bickerings of his contemporaries, and if once his calm was ruffled by one of the Titans of his day, it was as though an Olympian, intolerably provoked, had reluctantly, almost wearily, launched his bolt and in an instant the offender lay scorched and blasted beneath mountains of shame and contempt. . . .

"There is about Newman the same harmony and completeness: he has the subtlety of Coleridge without his frailty, the vigour of Carlyle without his rudeness, the grace of Arnold without his superficiality, the beauty of Ruskin without his priggishness, the sanctity of his own comrades of the Oxford Movement without their narrowness. It may even be said that he had at any rate potentially the lyric ecstasy of Tennyson, for who shall venture to put even *Crossing the Bar* upon a higher level than *Lead Kindly Light* with its last two lines, whose depths no mortal plummet shall ever sound?"

As the Movement progressed, the State thought something must be done to signalise the Anglican Church abroad as Protestant and devised the mad scheme of a Bishopric in Jerusalem. For the first time the tense atmosphere of the Movement was broken by humour. A converted German Jew, baptised in England and consecrated by the Bishop of Kildare, was sent out to Jerusalem as "Bishop of the United Church of England and Ireland." The King of Lutheran Prussia joined in this hopeful enterprise and was called to sponsor the infant Prince of Wales in consequence. Bishop Alexander was not sent to conquer the East but to be friendly to the Greeks and to persuade the Jews. Gladstone and Hope Scott told the Primate that his functions could be better performed by a Consul. He brought his wife in a litter and entered the Holy City under the protection of the Pasha. The *Tablet* compared them to Antony and Cleopatra:

"On either side of her
  Stood pretty dimpled boys like smiling Cupids."

Kinglake, in *Eothen,* refers to their "pretty English nursemaids" as the principal Christian propaganda in Palestine at the time. On the other hand, Newmanites like John Wynne and the future Catholic Bishop Patterson went and surrendered in person to the Latin Patriarch in Jerusalem. Bishop Alexander's importance was that the Jerusalem Bishopric pushed Newman towards Rome. It was the beginning of the end. Alexander died the month after Newman's conversion, Providence perhaps having no further use for him. It was brought against Newman that he had never read German, or religious history would have been different in England. It may now be reckoned for righteousness to him that he rejected a spiritual *entente* with the Prussian State.

Another bold move was the planting of an Anglican Church outside the very gates of Rome. This pathetic protest against idolatry remained outside the *Porta di Populo,* for the Pope could still keep Rome clear of heresy. It was oriented North by South to the distress of a later and High Church incumbent, who had to turn to the wall to take the Eastward position. King Edward was once present and humourously suggested that the Compass should be traced in front of the Altar.

Once that the Tractarians were a power, they were challenged from the Protestant and Liberal sides. When a Tractarian, Isaac Williams, stood for the Professorship of Poetry, the Battle of Books became a Battle of Sects. The University preferred a bad poet to a bad Protestant, so Williams, a Welsh bard but a follower of Newman, was defeated. His *Autobiography,* one of the few lucid and readable pictures of the early Movement, describes the reign of terror to which his supporters were subjected. One man voted against him because he had heard that drinking parties had ceased in Oxford since the Tractarians!

A stronger challenge came with the Memorial raised to the Oxford Martyrs, which Newman's friends wished to oppose or avoid, for it was erected to spite the Catholic party. The Tractarians were more successful in condemning Dr. Hampden, who was considered a Rationalist when lecturing as Professor of Divinity. The Liberals had their revenge when Pusey was suspended for High Church preaching and the State came to the side of the Liberals and made Hampden Bishop of Hereford. He was said to be the only Aristotelian in Oxford, and if all men are Aristotelians or Platonists the Tractarians were the latter. He and Newman represented the two poles of opinion: one afraid of infidelity and the other of over-credulity.

Hampden was a feeble match for Newman. His whole importance was that the Tractarians had been looking for a Liberal on whom to flesh their newly cut teeth. The Liberals immediately used him as a mitred missile. Whately alone could have withstood Newman in those days but he had retired to Dublin. The great Arnold was brought to Oxford to disperse Newman's imaginations from the Chair of History, but after making his prelude, suddenly died. Arnold, according to Church, was "Newman's great opposite." But only Newman could depose Newman from Oxford.

The first Tracts seemed too innocent and their writers too well-meaning to stir strife, but their effect was so marked and immoderate that counter-reply assumed fiercer shape. Arnold had denounced "the Oxford malignants" and Whately had written of them as "children of the mist." He even drew a touching parallel between Tractarians and Thugs. Maurice, the first Christian Socialist, spoke of escape as from "a charmed dungeon." Robertson, the brilliant preacher, wrote of "the paralyzing effects of the Oxford delusion." Mark Pattison said that "the Tracts desolated Oxford life" since everybody became a theologian. Kingsley wrote grimly that the Tracts contained "moaning piety and something darker." And in the underworld of Protestantism the sediment of ages was stirred to the dregs.

Meanwhile the Bishops rocked nervously between the two parties and supplied "the sharp sarcasms and kind cautions" which established hens have always served to ducklings threatening to embark on a new element. The Tractarians in their enthusiasm insisted that their Bishops were swans and should join them in the rushing stream. By 1845 Archbishop Howley had issued a Charge calling for no changes. Innovators had not done wrong, while those who had not innovated remained right. Bishop Blomfield, with infinite ingenuity, ordered the Popish surplice for morning and the Genevan gown for afternoon use. Candles might be used but not lit. Howley was born in the year of the Stamp Act which lost America

JOHN KEBLE
(From a portrait made July 24, 1863)

and was Bishop of London before Waterloo. Harcourt, Archbishop of York, was a nonagenarian born in the reign of George II. He was translated to York the year that Cardinal Stuart of York died. Both were venerable fossils who were shocked by the Movement. But Newman carried the youth and chivalry of Oxford. Afterwards Dean Lake wrote: "They all come back to this that the one great power which then ruled and inspired Oxford was Newman. The only persons, who were left outside the charmed circle, were the twenty Heads of Houses and a few Tutors, of whom Tait was the only one of power." Principal Shairp recalled: "They had shown a new thing in Oxford and England: had turned their backs on preferment and promotion and given their lives to what worldlings called a hopeless enterprise."

Of the Tutors, two Fellows of Balliol were rivals with contrasting views, Tait and Ward. Ward became Tennyson's pet Ultramontane, a real theologian, a music-loving buffoon with a logical way of asking Newman awkward questions. He had prompted Tract 90. As Dean Church wrote: "The agitations of Newman's mind were reinforced by the impulses of Mr. Ward's." He took Hurrell Froude's place in setting the pace to the reluctant leader. He invented the phrase *credo in Newmannum* but his *Magnificat* was dedicated to himself. He was a reckless self-advertiser and insisted on riding the crest of the wave. He wrote his *Ideal of a Christian Church* to shock Oxford. When he claimed to hold the full cycle of Roman doctrine in the Church of England he received the picturesque fall he desired. A thousand members of the University met to deprive him of his Degrees in February,

1845. Newman stayed away, for the next item was the Condemnation of Tract 90, which was only prevented by the historic Veto of the Proctors. All this took place amid a storm of counter-cheering and hooting. Authorities never dared meet Newman or Pusey face to face, but always endeavoured to condemn them behind their backs.

This year brought the end. Wiseman had sent Father Bernard Smith to Littlemore, who reported that Newman was already wearing light-coloured trousers and therefore could no longer entertain belief in Anglican Orders. Newman began writing his *Essay on Development.* Not only did he trace the whole past of the Church from the oak back to the acorn, but a wrong interpretation of his statement was to aid in breeding a distant Modernism.

While he wrote the *Essay,* he drifted into the arms of Rome. His own master-hand has described the over-mastering scene. Even in his *Apologia* he could not recall the thousand subtleties driving him forward or back. He had reached a time when he felt responsible equally for disciples who went over to Rome and for those who stayed. When Lockhart, his Curate, went over on a pilgrimage to St. Gilbert of Sempringham, he had resigned St. Mary's. In the last stages he was influenced by the fates of his friends. At last a simple Italian Passionist arrived and received the over-subtle one out of his misery. It is said that the guard on the coach asked the traveller to remember him. "I will remember you in my Mass," said the simple one. Newman's last night in Oxford was spent at the Observatory with friends. There the light of the *Stella Maris* befell him.

When Newman withdrew to Littlemore he had lived

in the twilight between two worlds. He had turned to the dead, and as though he dared not use the *ora pro nobis,* he devised the *oret pro nobis* to win the prayers of the Saints. His friends gathered about him as men appointed to die. He had preached his farewell sermon to Pusey's sobs. Even so he was feared if he put brick upon brick. One lonely man seemed to be rebuilding all the Abbeys of England. When he went over to Rome, there were many who preferred to be wrong with Plato than ascend to Heaven or to the House of Lords with Archbishop Howley. Mark Pattison wrote that it was "impossible to describe the enormous effect in the Academical and Clerical world by one man's changing his religion. But it was not consternation. It was a lull."

A few days after Newman's secession the poet Clough wrote: "The poet Faber men say will go, but the ultra-Puseyites seem inclined not to take headers like Ward, but to sneak in and duck their heads till they are out of their depth." The Protestants could hoist the egregious banner of "I told you so" over the University. In the following year Freeman recorded a violent attack on the Blessed Virgin in her own Church from Dr. Jeune, a College Head.

The stream of the Movement divided against the Rock but it flowed and has continued to flow as strongly on one side as the other. From that day both Anglican and Roman Churches were re-created in England. The Oxford Movement in its first phase was over.

III

THE SECOND PHASE

The Church of England approached the mid-century with Pusey and Wilberforce at the helm and Manning on the look-out. "Safe as Manning" became a watchword. Manning, now Archdeacon of Chichester, was working hand in glove with Gladstone. The idea of Colonial Bishoprics and the beginnings of Pan-Anglicanism were his. Ten Bishoprics were not enough for a Seventh of the globe he noted, and he called on Anglicans to be "almoners to a lost world." He differenced the Churches by saying that Rome was irregular in Doctrine but Canterbury in Discipline. The latter was therefore preferable.

Manning was only defeated over the Gorham case. Bishop Philpotts of Exeter refused to institute Gorham, who disbelieved in Grace at Baptism. Gorham put his trust in the Privy Council which righted him by a decision from Jenner Fust, one of the famous ecclesiastical lawyers who commenced to settle rite and doctrine for Anglicans. Fust settled the famous case of *Connelly* vs. *Connelly,* between a Catholic Priest and his former Anglican wife. He gave it against the Roman law of conjugal separation. At Rome the Gorham case would have been settled in twenty minutes, but the Anglican Church was distracted for a year and the Bishop of Exeter ceased Communion with the Primate. The story is that after a stern meeting Philpotts threatened to pray for Archbishop Howley, who turned pale and said "anything but that!" Manning resigned his Archdeaconry and surrendered to Rome. The controversy whether a man may marry his Deceased Wife's Sister could also have been settled by Roman Canon Law but it needed an Act of Parliament to conclude the fifty years of controversy. One distracted lady said she wished Gorham would marry his Deceased Wife's Sister and be done with it!

Manning's action was appreciated by Wiseman, who was moving in a dream and reordained the Archdeacon in six weeks. Anglican and Roman camps were equally perturbed by this rapid transit between altars. Manning was acting not only under the negation of the Gorham controversy but under the positive return of the Catholic Hierarchy.

In 1851 the Pope felt strong enough to make a move towards his beloved *Angli*. The First Gregory had converted them and the Sixteenth never heard the word *Inghilterra* without weeping. Pius IX no more understood *Angli* or *Anglicani* than his predecessors or successors, being dependent on the hearsay of Latin travellers or the excited gossip of Converts. For instance, De Lisle, with his A. P. U.C. or Association for the Promotion of Union of Christendom (sometimes rendered A Plaster for Unquiet Consciences!), talked of thousands of Clergy and even Bishops being ready to come over. When Pius restored the Hierarchy with Cardinal Wiseman at the head, England went mad and 6,000 meetings were held in protest. There was always a strong belief in England that the Pope was

the Antichrist of Revelations. Renan had not yet explained
that Antichrist was Nero, while Sir Isaac Newton had
slyly observed that the Pope had the bad luck to be very
like him! Lord Shaftesbury thought Lord John Russell's
answer to Wiseman "worthy of Cromwell's defiance of
the Duke of Savoy." Thackeray said the only answer was
to elect an Anglican Bishop over the Palatine Hill. Nevertheless there was a movement in the 'Fifties to Rome: Mas-
kell, Dodsworth, Neville, and Anderdon, all outstanding
men, Stephenson the Historian, Archdeacon Wilberforce,
Sergeant Bellasis, Sir John Simeon, William Palmer the
Orientalist, Pollen the Senior Proctor. Neither in '45 nor in
'51 was there any stampede. It was a falling and disappear-
ing as of ripened fruits.

Conversion to Rome was not a fashion then or a literary
event or an æsthetic gesture. Men on both sides suffered
intensely, both mentally and physically. Bishop Wilberforce fell into a fever and remained sleepless while his
brother and brother-in-law were passing. Pusey, who had
sobbed through Newman's farewell sermon on the parting of friends, only desired to be allowed to lie down and
die during the exodus of 1851. Allies compared leaving
the Church of England to Abraham's sacrifice of Isaac.
Looking back he wrote: "I feel like the man who rode
his horse over a bridge of boats one night and when he
saw what he had done next day died of fright." Men were
serious on either side and religious arguments, which could
not cause more than a week's dismay or annoyance to-day,
were followed by life-long enmities and separations.

The fate of the early Converts has often been a subject

of pity or surmise. Roughly there were 500 from Oxford and 200 from Cambridge. Most of them drifted into mundane oblivion but many were too able to go under and founded corners of activity or circles of Grace. Manning became harnessed to Wiseman's chariot and founded a House of St. Charles in Bayswater. During the Crimean War he was supplying Chaplains and sending nursing Sisters to Florence Nightingale, whom he had nearly brought over to Rome. Newman, meantime, was lecturing on the Turks in Europe. He had withdrawn to Birmingham and founded his Oratory. He had explained their difficulties most truly even though rather cruelly to Anglicans by analysing and probing his nursing mother. As it were, he dissected the breasts from which he had drunk. He had found her nutrition void and her milk a delusion. It was pathetic how Anglicans always clung to his memory. They sang his Hymns and read, when they could no longer hear, his Sermons. It is interesting to add Dean Stanley's selection, made for sheer beauty, from their number:

"The Sorrows of Human Life in the Sermon on Bethseda,"
"Elijah on Mount Horeb,"
"St. Peter's Arrival in Rome,"
"The Description of Dives,"
"The Agony in the Garden,"
"The Growth of Belief in the Assumption of the Virgin."

Imagine these pronounced in a slow mysterious voice, every syllable melodious as drops of water on a marble fountain. Only the future can reveal whether Newman was as great a theologian as a writer. After studying his thirty-six volumes Lionel Johnson discovered incidentally: "the truest estimates of Byron and of Cicero: the best theory of portrait painting: the subtlest description of musical emotion: books more full than Thackeray's of worldly knowledge."

The Catholic Newman wrote neither as a Gallican nor Ultramontane in days when the Church preferred partisans. When his subtle English was translated into Italian, he was often misunderstood at Rome. It is difficult to say which treated him worse, the Irish Bishops, who borrowed his services in Dublin, or the English Hierarchy, who dispensed with them for Oxford. It was his ever-thwarted desire to return to the city where he had been an uncrowned King, or rather an unmitred Bishop. Before the British public could forget Newman's existence, Kingsley stated that he was presumably in favour of lying and the *Apologia* burst forth like a concealed flame.

After Newman's disappearance the Liberals had Oxford to themselves. It was against Liberals more than Protestants that Newman had declared war. It was a while before the discomfited Pusey and Keble could pick up shield or buckler. Their spearsman was in the Roman Legion.

When Newman left, there was a lull as though after the falling of a great tree in the forest. The sound of drifting leaves continued a long time after: the hurrying sound of those who followed him or were scattered further afield. It is not realised how disturbing the Movement had proved to men's souls. Jowett said: "many fine characters and good intellects were shipwrecked." A lost Tractarian was the poet Clough, whom Ward had pushed to the edge between Rome or nothing: *Aut Papa aut nullus.* Clough fell into nothing. Others saved themselves by a fierce bitterness. Froude never ceased to write with gall and acid, with the good result of rousing the High Church historians Freeman and Stubbs who called Pusey "master." Brewer, another piece of flotsam from the Movement, devoted himself to Calendaring Henry VIII, whom Froude tried to canonise as a splendid mixture of David and Saul, and the perfect Protestant English gentleman! Mark Pattison left his *Memoirs* to be published like a posthumous sling. They are best read page by page with Newman's *Apologia*. Both men were egotists, but there the parallel ceased. Pattison incidentally accused Pusey of betraying his confession, which sounds incredible.

The Tractarians set about founding Public Schools, finding how irreligious education was even at Schools like Eton and Winchester which dated from Catholic days. Radley, Bradfield, and Lancing were formed in an attempt to bring the Middle Ages to the sons of the Middle Classes. Woodard, the principal spirit behind the new foundations, lies enshrined in the magnificent Chapel at Lancing. Sewell, who founded Radley, started St. Columba's for the Anglo-Irish. Gladstone and Hope Scott set out to found Glenalmond in Scotland. The old Schools had been revolutionised by Dr. Arnold of Rugby and, though bitterly anti-Tractarian, he had made the School Chapel part of the life of England. Eton could hardly be called High, but it was traditional compared to Evangelical Harrow. Yet from Harrow came Manning and Faber and three

Catholic Bishops. Eton produced the great Anglican leaders Pusey, Canon Carter, and Lord Halifax. Eton has since given Rome as many converts as all the other Schools together. A Puseyite wave ebbed surreptitiously through the School sweeping up sentimental boys and Masters. Allies, Wynne, and Pollen were notable Old Etonian converts and two masters, Walford and Kegan Paul, passed over, leaving their colleague Cory to write "to the Infallible":

"Old angler, what device is thine
　　To draw my pleasant friends from me?
Thou fishest with a silken line
　　Not the coarse nets of Galilee."

Poetical boys like Dolben and Bridges looked forward to becoming monks. Dolben was drowned on the verge of the Church but Bridges lived to become Laureate.

The day of Jowett and the Broad Church was coming. Oxford politics flowed in vicious circles. Pusey had once prevented Jowett's marriage, when he asked leave from a Committee of Heads of Colleges. Jowett was thwarted of Tutorship as a Newmanite suspect and of Balliol Mastership as a Liberal. Pusey preached a series against Jowett's *Essay on Atonement*. Palmerson made Jowett a Professor to score off the Church and Jowett was handed the Thirty-Nine Articles by a Vice-Chancellor who expected protest. Jowett signed with hurried scorn. Plato was his God and Christ a great Philosopher. He permitted doubt but penalised Atheism. On a celebrated occasion he gave an undergraduate so many hours in which to find God or be rusticated. Jowett's was the winning influence and Balliol finally came under his sway. W. H. Mallock, who eventually became a Catholic, described the Balliol school thus: "Their denials of everything, which to me had been previously sacred, appalled me like the overture to some approaching tragedy. Their confident attempts at some new scheme of affirmations affected me like a solemn farce." The Broad Church germinated from Stanley's *Life of Arnold* and ended in Dean Farrar's *Life of Christ*. Jowett confessed that God had not given him power to write the *Life of Christ* which was left to Farrar. In spite of its success Farrar complained of the small sum he had received and was reminded that he only merited thirty pieces of silver. Stanley became Dean of Westminster, where he revived the Abbey Sanctuary in favour of any harassed heretic or persecuted Modernist. Stanley was an English Renan. He had no use for miracles or the Divinity in Christ, but he was always fair to Catholics. Together with Tait on the Commission of Enquiry he helped to take the starch out of clerical Oxford, while poor Pusey seemed to mistake Privilege for Principle. Graduates no longer had to sign the Articles.

When Stanley offered the Abbey-pulpit to Pusey he was told that they held no single truth in common "except that somehow Jesus came from God which the Mohammedan believes too." Pusey threw olive branches to Rome but he kept a barge pole for the Liberals of the Broad Church. Pusey's ecclesiastical fortunes were strange. Inhibited by his Bishop except in the village of Pusey, he was allowed two pulpits in London. Yet he was powerful enough to save the Athanasian Creed from Liberal tampering by the mere threat of his secession.

In 1860 the Broad Churchmen published *Essays and Reviews,* which impugned Scriptural accuracy and threw cold water on eternal damnation. The Reviewers, assailed as *Septem contra Christum,* included Jowett and Pattison, the future Archbishop Temple and Wilson, one of the Tutors who had moved against Tract 90. High and Low Church kissed in holy hatred of them. Wilberforce called on them to resign in honesty. The Court of Arches condemned two of the Essayists to suspension and by a stroke of Nemesis Wilson was condemned for having "suggested modes by which the Articles may be evaded," which had been his accusation against Newman. The Essayists appealed to the Privy Council, who reversed the Court of Arches, while Lord Chancellor Westbury "dismissed eternal punishment with costs!" This Pusey called a "miserable soul-destroying Judgment," but Pusey's strength was revealed when he collected the signatures of 11,000 Clergy.

In the midst of the fracas came trouble from Africa, the grave of Churches and Dynasties. Bishop Colenso of Natal, under the questioning of Zulus, lost faith in the accuracy of Moses. He could not even use the Baptismal Service because it alluded to the Flood, of which there was then no proof in archæology. The Zulus could not believe in Noah's floating Zoo and Colenso agreed with them. He was excommunicated by his Metropolitan, Gray of Capetown, and appealed to the blessed Privy Council, which was becoming the deciding and teaching power in the Lambeth Patriarchate. The Privy Council justified the Bishop and the battle of Colenso continued. Gray had the courage to consecrate a successor to Natal when the home

Bishops hesitated. "Either the Privy Council destroys the Church or vice versa," remarked the Archbishop. The Privy Council would not allow one School to turn another out of the Church. Colenso returned home and when refused an Oxford pulpit by Wilberforce preached in Balliol. The judgment for Colenso proved the Freedom of the Colonial Churches.

Meantime, in spite of Commission and Reform, the Church of England made a bid to hold Oxford. The Bishop thereof, Wilberforce, to all ages known as "Soapy Sam," was the typical High State and Church Bishop, who stood in the gap and charged equally against Newman and the Essayists, against Higher Critic and Ritualist. He attributed his nickname to keeping his fingers clean in spite of the hot water they constantly encountered. His enemy, the Chancellor Westbury, attributed it to "saponacious" reasons. His greater enemy, Disraeli, gave the Primacy to Tait and barred Wilberforce from the promotion which he had both deserved and desired. To add insult to injury he caricatured him in *Lothair* as the Bishop who vainly tried to secure Lord Bute from the seductions of Rome. He is summarised bitterly and well in Allies' *Life's Decision*. Allies was an Eton Newcastle scholar, whose *Journal* Sam wished to condemn, but the wiser Pusey and Manning had prevented its coming to judgment. Allies became a Catholic and wrote the *Formation of Christendom* in seven volumes. Being neither an historian nor a stylist, his answer to Gibbon remains a mighty might-have-been.

The Church of England was held together by a wise dispensation of patronage. Comprehension was sought as well as compromise. The old Bishops had not the imagination or Grace to realise the dynamic power behind the new Movement. Wilberforce knew it too well and was inclined to use Pusey as his sheep dog. Pusey was called the Church-Bell by the Romans, since he rang others to Rome but never entered the door himself. Wilberforce was distracted in many directions. He tilted against Huxley and gave Disraeli the famous occasion to say he was on the side of the Angels rather than of the monkeys. Wilberforce went bald-headed against Science, but Pusey had made his peace with a power he foresaw might become a weapon against the Church. Back in the 'Forties he had lent his stables for experiments and influenced the Church vote to build the Museum out of monies made by printing the Bible. The child of Light was as wise as the children of Science.

Wilberforce entirely changed the aspect and aspirations of Anglican Bishops. When pious duplicity was deemed a constant necessity, he bore the odium of playing two parts. He had protested against Hampden's Bishopric, but retreated to soft pedalling. He allowed the Ritualists to advance under his capacious sleeves, though he called them "mowing apes." He won and lost favour at Court, for the Prince Consort suspected him of wishing to tutor the young Prince. He held Oxford for the Anglicans against both Liberals and Romans, whom he assailed as a "debased communion." He stood in the gap at the parting of many ways and the Church of England owes to him whatever she was able to learn of statecraft. But her priestcraft, in a laudable sense, she learnt of Pusey. Wilberforce could debate and wrangle with the State, though he was not great enough to break the ever-eating fetter of State Control.

After the Gorham Judgment there had been a proposal to assert freedom from the State and to get Pusey, Manning, and Keble consecrated Bishops, but without rectifying their Orders, by a Greek or Jansenist Bishop. After Manning's secession Keble and Pusey retreated to their Anglican shell.

The promoters of Reunion in Christendom, which was based on the Branch theory, kept up a shower of leafless olive branches. The Holy Office condemned the Branch theory and Manning became Archbishop. His policy was to allow no terms but retraction. Explanations, conciliation, and reunion he scouted. The Reunionists were driven between the Devil and the Holy See. Under Dr. Lee of Lambeth they took a startling but logical step. Lee with two allies in Anglican Orders, Mossman and Seccombe, was secretly reordained as "Bishop of Dorchester" by a Greek Bishop in the Adriatic. They returned to England and secretly reordained and reconfirmed a great many hesitants. In the end both Lee and Mossman passed into communion with Rome. The Order of Corporate Reunion was promulgated on the steps of St. Paul's Cathedral to the initiated, no doubt while the Dean slept. But it was never known to what extent they had distributed valid Orders amongst their friends. Officially neither Rome nor Canterbury knew anything about it. All was conducted under the Seal of Confession and all names have been kept secret till this day.

Still Anglicans held their battered Church together. Convocation of Clergy was revived the year after Manning's secession. From 1717 to 1852 Convocation was not a working assembly. In the days of Queen Anne it had been the battle-ground between Whig Bishops and the Hig Church Clergy under the ranting Dr. Sacheverell. Church Bells had been dedicated to God and Sacheverell. The Church of England, having no Popes, always fell back upon champions like Dean Swift, Sacheverell, and Pusey, who were seldom Bishops.

High Churchmen were persecuted if they were weak, but if they showed the strength likely to follow Manning, they were made Bishops. Keble's Curate, for instance, was for years denied priesthood because he was Keble's Curate. Forbes and Kerr Hamilton, on the other hand, were made Bishops of Brechin and Salisbury from the ranks of the Anglican Highest. High Churchmen became very stubborn. Keble declared that if the Church of England failed elsewhere it would be found in his Parish. Pusey at the London anti-Gorham meeting declared that as words would not convince men of his fidelity to his Church, "death in her bosom will." Gladstone kept converts from Rome.

In the public eye the main result of the Oxford Movement was the strife engendered between High and Low Church. Riots, liturgical brawls, and lawsuits followed endlessly. A volume would be needed to describe the slow, fighting triumph of the High. They always had the life and youth of the rising Church with them against the dead letter of the law which sheltered the Low. The Trac-

EDWARD BOUVERIE PUSEY, D.D.

(From a portrait by Miss Rosa Corder. The *Life of Edward Bouverie Pusey*, Longmans, Green, & Co.)

tarians were not Ritualists. Newman found and left nap-
kins on the altar of St. Mary's and consecrated North-
wards. At Littlemore there were two candlesticks and a
gentle lifting of hands at the Consecration, with slight
bendings towards the Cross. But those, who stayed in the
Church of England, were determined to temper their loyalty by forbidden rites. Vestments were adopted here and
there as far back as the 'Forties and Canon Chamberlain
and J. M. Neale restored the chasuble, when even the surplice was perilous to wear. Mr. Courtenay was mobbed in
his surplice at Exeter in 1845 and died of his emotions.

The Ritualists used their flaming mantle to provoke
John Bull, while reserving the sword of doctrine to touch
his obstinate heart. Both High and Low went steadily to
law. The Church Association obtained sixty condemna-
tions against the High. So great and expensive was the
legal work that it led to a religious revival amongst the
lawyers. The High founded the secret Society of the Holy
Cross and the English Church Union, which fought their
battles in the Courts. They found the famous Ornaments
Rubric was in their favour, for it specified the use of the
ornaments during the second year of Edward VI, which
included the vestments. The Bishops became buffers between High and Low and between Convocation and Parliament. The Royal Commission of 1867 afforded a life-
boat in contrary seas. Vestments were thereby restricted,
not prohibited.

It was discovered that the Low Church were not keeping the letter of the law either. If the High strained the
sense of the Articles, the Low were inclined to rub out

Rubrics. One Bishop laid down: "Avoid Ritual and preach any doctrine you like!" But both Parties put their honour above Rubrics. Wordsworth seemed to have prophesied for the best:

"Watchwords of Party on all tongues are rife
  As if a Church, though sprung from Heaven, must owe
  To opposites and fierce extremes her life."

Tractarians who remained in the Church of England felt they had the right to illuminate the Tracts with Ritualism. The Puseyites selected St. Thomas the Martyr in Oxford as a field for pious experiment. Pioneers took up their positions with very different fates ahead: Brian King, at St. George's in the East, Bennett, at St. Paul's Knightsbridge, and Dr. Neale, at East Grinstead. Oakeley went to All Saints in Margaret Street, whence he passed to Rome. Pioneer Churches became besieged Citadels. At St. Andrew's, Well Street, a chorister was wounded to death and commemorated in stained glass. For a year Brian King officiated amid howling mobs. He withdrew shattered, leaving Father Lowder to make St. Peter's, London Docks, famous in the Anglican world. Amid scenes of poverty and neglect the High Churchmen built up Church order and beauty. St. Peter's, Vauxhall, was built on the site of an infamous resort. It was the same at the mission which Bennett founded at St. Barnabas', Pimlico. He was driven out of London and at Frome made St. John's the most ornate Church in the Provinces. Dr. Brett, a layman, founded church after church on the London borders, working from St. Matthias at Stoke Newington, of which the first Vicar, Father Pope, became an Oratorian. All these men were subjected to scenes like the French Revolution. The tail end of the mob which brought Laud to the scaffold howled through the 'Fifties and 'Sixties. Pusey built St. Saviour's in Leeds, with a College of celibate parsons, who seceded in two groups Romeward, including a future Catholic Bishop, Wilkinson of Hexham. The Bishop of Ripon baited the unhappy Pollen, who proposed to teach Seven Sacraments to the people, who previously had none. Dr. Hook, the Vicar, became almost insane with fury and his cries rose above even the shrieks of the mob. Poor Pusey was well used to bowing to storms. "It is really cruel, mere Jesuitism, it is wicked. Oh Pusey, do seek for simplicity of mind." Hook was happier dealing with dead Archbishops than with lively Curates, and withdrew to write the *Lives of the Primates.*

The first Tractarian churches are forgotten. The battles which raged over them have passed into oblivion. They have been long surpassed by others in ritual. The congregations which filled them in the spirit of the Catacombs as well as the bluff No-Popery mobs are no longer conceivable. Their names remain like the corners of a battlefield, which only the dead combatants could feel beating in their blood.

From London the thirst for Ritual spread through the Provinces. At St. Peter's, Plymouth, Father Prynne restored the Daily Eucharist. He was exonerated after a libel lawsuit over the Confessional and had to sell his wife's wedding presents to pay the costs. In dull Unitarian Birmingham the brothers Pollock restored Catholic service. At Brighton the Wagners built five High Churches, one of which gave rise to the Purchas Judgment sanctioning Vestments, to be reversed by the Privy Council. The fight never left the Lawcourts. From St. Peter's, London Docks, Father Mackonochie came to St. Alban's, Holborn, and there Dean Stanley saw "three men in green who will yet give us trouble." Incense and Dalmatics had already appeared at St. Mary Magdalen's, Munster Square, but St. Alban's carried out the full High Mass. A generation of lawsuits followed during which every point except incense was at one time declared legal and at another illegal. Incense, which was the only point which could be proved from Scripture, was oddly enough the one illegality which stuck most in John Bull's windpipe. No Bishop would consecrate the Holy Oils, so Mackonochie performed the act himself. Later the Oils for the use of the Church of England were sent by registered mail from the hands of a Bishop of America. In the ecclesiastical world oil appeared to be thicker than water.

In 1868 the Privy Council condemned lighted candles at the Communion by the casting vote of the Archbishop of York, whereat Wilberforce recorded: "It is a very serious thing to have the Supreme Court decide to satisfy the public and not as the Law really is." After his death this remark appeared in his *Life,* whereat the Queen was petitioned to publish an official contradiction.

Famous judgments and notorious names have perished in the dust of long ago. But we can still sympathise with Mr. Purchas, who was condemned for twenty-nine illegal practices, and rather than face the costs of trial made over his fortune to his wife. Of all the points most fiercely debated, there was one which never came up for judgment, the celibacy of the Clergy, perhaps because Dr. Pusey had been married. The bulk of the High Church had followed his laudable example. It was encouraged by the Bishops, for seceders to Rome were generally celibates. The despairing cry of a would-be convert is recorded that he had only thirteen reasons against Rome: his wife and twelve children! For all that, many celibates remained Anglican, while married clergy often brought their children and poverty into the Catholic Church. It has been pointed out that Greek Priests in union with Rome have remained married and it has consequently been suggested than an Anglican Uniate Church might, if its Orders were adjusted, keep an English Service and their wives.

In 1872 came the Bennett Case, in which the Privy Council gave permission for the Real Presence in the Church of England! It was the reverse of the story of the Jansenist sanctuary, in which God was officially forbidden to perform miracles! The Church Association, which had fought nobly for the Real Absence, suffered defeat accordingly. The battle of the Eucharist was waged in St. Alban's, Holborn, where Father Mackonochie led the ritual advance and cost the English Church Union 10,000 pounds sterling. A dogged Scotchman; he cared no more for English Bishops than any Covenanter. He conquered by sheer will and self-sacrifice.

Lord Shaftesbury was a horrified visitor to his Church in 1866, where he vividly described: "the worship of Jupiter and Juno . . . theatrical gymnastics . . . clouds upon clouds of incense, the censer frequently refreshed by the

High Priest who kissed the spoon as he dug out the sacred powder!"

The power of the Evangelicals had lain in their philanthropy. After William Wilberforce, Hannah More, and Howard, Shaftesbury proved a fanatical and fearless champion. Disraeli called him a "vain maniac," but his achievement in protecting the children and women in the mines is written in the Book of Life. His religious fury is another question and is historical, for he led the opposition of Parliament and People against the Oxford Movement. At College he had read Aristotle with Pusey, but they came to "differ intensely and fearfully on points of unspeakable importance." Needless to say, Shaftesbury had blessed the Jerusalem Bishopric and cursed the Tractarians. Curiously enough both Archdeacon Manning and Sam Wilberforce had favoured the Jerusalem scheme which cut the Anglican ropes out of Newman's clinging hands. Pusey realised that it afforded the first occasion that the Church of England held communion with those outside their Church, but Shaftesbury was delighted with the High Church wrath and wrote: "We must build a new ward for the Puseyites in Bedlam." Shaftesbury's mentality can be guessed from his belief that the Government ship conveying the Bishop was one of the "ships of Tarshish" of prophecy. In the fight for the Chair of Poetry at Oxford, rather than admit a Tractarian (though it had been Shakespeare or Spenser), he would vote for a Brady and Tate or any pious mangler of the Psalmist. He preferred to believe that England was always saved at sea not by the strong hand of her sailors but by the weather provided by a Protestant God: in 1588, in 1719, and 1798. On those occasions "bad visibility" fought for England. He fought the High Church with the combined power of the State, the Law, and his brother-in-law, the Prime Minister Palmerston. This cynical rake was wisely content to let the good Lord Shaftesbury become Bishop-maker. Jowett described Bishop-making as "giving great prizes for moderation and sometimes for dishonesty." When Aberdeen fell, Wilberforce lamented that "the only Government fair to the Church had been overthrown over the lack of a road from Balaclava to Sebastopol." Wilberforce and the Bishops manœuvred against Shaftesbury, but he created a long series of Low Church Bishops and Deans including Longley of Canterbury and Thomson of York. Except for Tait not a name of them has survived save in the D.N.B. or Dictionary of No Bodies sometimes called. Wilberforce deplored "Pam's wicked appointments" and rejoiced when the "Bishop-maker was dethroned by the fall of Pam." Both High and Broad were opposed to Low Church nonentities and asked for "learned" appointments, which might more possibly cloak their own doctrines. Palmerston was content with Bishoprics which won him votes in the country. If he sent Bickersteth to Ripon, it was to adjust the balance between Oxford and Cambridge on the Bench! Gladstone chafed under Palmerston, only begging him to make Jacobson Bishop of Chester as his political Chairman and vital to his Oxford seat. But the High Church could not save Gladstone and he was eventually swept out at the threat of Irish Disestablishment. To Shaftesbury's indignation Jacobson was High enough to withdraw his sanction from the Bible Society. Gladstone as Premier entered into his Kingdom and made High Church appointments, tempered by the choice of Temple for Exeter. Shaftesbury and Pusey united against this Modernist, but the confusion amongst Evangelical Deans appears in a letter of Shaftesbury:

"The Dean of Gloucester joins Pusey and protests against Temple and Pusey, and the Dean of Exeter joins Temple and protests against everyone who differs from him. Who is to lead a regiment like that? Even Falstaff would not march through Coventry with them."

Shaftesbury and Pusey united again in defence of the Athanasian Creed against the Modernists. Shaftesbury was delighted with Pusey's book which defended the Prophet Daniel with erudite vigour. Daniel was, of course, a great hero with those who believed that he foretold the Papacy in unpleasant colours. When Seeley's *Ecce Homo* appeared, like an English version of Renan's *Vie de Jesus,* Shaftesbury denounced it as "the most pestilential book ever vomited out of the jaws of Hell." Shaftesbury's power failed under Gladstone and Disraeli, but he remained the Evangelical Hercules, who as far as one man was able hindered the Oxford Movement. His apocalyptic screams echo through the discussions of his time and he deserves credit for averting revolution in the country though not in his Church.

Disraeli made Church appointments solely to win votes. He was upset to find himself opposed by the disgusted High Church and appealed to Wilberforce, who pointed out "the bareness of an ostracised position," which they had enjoyed under Palmerston. Disraeli rode the Protestant horse in the Boroughs and, when he found the County elections endangered, whipped round and proposed any High Churchmen he could think of. Wilberforce confessed hating him till he could hate him no more, and not merely because he had cheated him of London and Canterbury. "More odious than Laud," reported Disraeli of Sam to the Queen. Gladstone's power came too late and could only console him with Winchester. If Wilberforce had not been killed in a fall from his horse, in 1872, no doubt Gladstone would have sent him to Canterbury ten years later.

The greatest layman evolved by the Movement was Gladstone. He was saturated with the religious questions raised at Oxford and the key to his life was theological. This accounts for the pitiable failure made of his *Life* by Lord Morley, which is Hamlet with Hamlet's melancholy omitted. Gladstone's whole career was staked, not on the Tory or Liberal Party being right, but on the Church of England being the Catholic Church in the land. In 1838, the year in which Wellington bluntly announced "the real question is Church or no Church," Gladstone wrote a book that read like an interminable speech to the grand old toast of Church and King. He claimed that the State had a conscience and was bound to uphold its Anglican expression, which drew a long, patronising and sarcastic Essay from Macaulay. In point of practice Gladstone resigned office rather than endow Maynooth, for the Tractarians insisted that the Anglo-Irish Church was the true Church of St. Patrick. In after years Gladstone described his act as "a notable projection from the ivory gate," but what was more to the point he reversed it by disestablishing the Irish Churchmen.

He had come under the Newman influence but after Tract 90 decided that Newman had burned his fingers. Time showed that he had burnt the High Church boats and Gladstone found refuge in the Ark provided by Archdeacon Manning. Palmer's Treatise on the Church and Manning's influence made him a High Churchman. Side by side he and Manning had advanced towards the highest posts in Church and State until the day of their tragic parting at a Communion Service. Gladstone proceeded to the altar but Manning remained on his knees. When Manning renounced his Archdeaconry, Gladstone felt that he had "murdered his mother." Compare Pusey's gentler suggestion that Newman in seceding had only been transferred to another part of the Lord's Vineyard.

The Oxford Movement disestablished the Anglo-Irish Church. High Churchmen were not consistent. Salisbury finally voted for the Bill which Gladstone introduced. The best defence was uttered by Magee, the Irish Bishop of Peterborough, who had once found the Orangemen too warm for him as Rector of Enniskillen. As soon as Gladstone mooted Irish disestablishment, Disraeli had moved Magee from an Irish deanery to an English See, to bring into play an orator who surpassed Gladstone. For the last time a Bishop's eloquence thrilled the House of Lords. Gladstone promoted Liddon, the acolyte of Pusey; Church, the historian of the Movement; and Kingsley, who had tried to disparage the greatest of the converts.

Before and after the Vatican Council Döllinger confirmed Gladstone in his Anglicanism. Gladstone suffered and even agonised with the Minority of the Council, who saw their hopes for an elastic Church destroyed. The dogma of Infallibility left little hope to Gallicans and none to Anglicans. Gladstone's bitter grief burst forth aloud in a Tract on *Vaticanism,* which might have been the speech of a Caroline Archbishop, could he have been present at the Council. He alluded to "the dark Syllabus" and "the myrmidons of the Apostolic See" in the finest Oxford debating style. He challenged English Catholics as bad citizens or bad Catholics henceforth and he reaped the thanks of Bismarck, for which he had as little appreciation as Bismarck for the subtleties of disappointed Anglicanism.

It was not the millinery or antics of the Ritualists that worried John Bull. In time he would have accepted them as a Sunday continuation of the Lord Mayor's Show. What grated on him was the Confessional, which with the Crinoline seemed subversive of the morality of the British female. To the English mind Confession is a sneaking against oneself. It was a serious and a secret matter for the High Churchmen. There is a story that the first lady to be confessed at Brighton was taken to an upper room and the blinds drawn, whereat the poor lady fell back in a fit. Wilberforce attacked Pusey over the Confessional because it was dreaded and unpopular, but Wilberforce himself was violently attacked when he defended a clergyman against a lady who would have qualified for the Order of Chastity in the Third Class. The *Times* in a leader and *Punch* in a caricature (Soapy Sam kissing the rod) fiercely criticised the Bishop over this Boyne Hill case. In 1873 nearly 500 parsons petitioned for Confessors' licenses. The alarmed Bishops debated but dared not decide on the abominable thing. In 1877 Lord Redesdale brought *The Priest in Absolution* before the Lords, the private manual of the Society of the Holy Cross. Though it only contained cautious advice on confessing young women, the Home Secretary declared it could be proceeded against as obscene. *Punch* issued a Cartoon on lines of savage self-righteousness. Bishops, Peers, and mob joined the outcry against the surpliced vipers, who even insinuated a suggestion against the virtue of the British female. Dean McNeile demanded Capital punishment for hearing Confessions. High Churchmen bowed before the storm which more nearly wrecked the Oxford Movement than the storm roused by Papal Aggression.

The Church Association lifted the Protestant flag and was cordially received by the Archbishops. Among its ranks was the new and Protestant Lord Shrewsbury. Another Peer, Lord Ebury, who lived for the cause of "securing purity and simplicity of worship in the Church of England," wished the Prayer Book to be revised, and Archbishop Tait supported him. The English Church Union, realising that they might lose the Catholic scraps in the liturgy, petitioned at that time to keep the Prayer Book as it was. Wilberforce wrote to Gladstone of "this counsel of fear which threatened destruction." Parliament was plagued with silly Bills. Lord Shaftesbury wished a fine of ten pounds to be imposed for wearing a Vestment. Others wanted altar lights and crosses confiscated and sold for the poor, which sounded like Judas' suggestion for using the Magdalen's spikenard. Ritual acts, such as a Bishop bearing a crosier, "must be reported by the Churchwardens to the Bishop who must forbid the same!" The Royal Commission on Ritual had been packed with High Churchmen and after three years and a hundred meetings left confusion worse confounded. Five years later John Bull lost his temper and put five parsons in gaol.

Only in England would a Divorce Judge, Lord Penzance, be put in charge of Ecclesiastical cases. Father Tooth, a Cambridge man, was the first to go to prison for the Oxford Movement. He was the Tooth *Punch* wished to have stopped, but he lived to celebrate the jubilee of his martyrdom. Mr. Enright was imprisoned and his consecrated wafer carried off as an exhibit, marked with pen and ink. Tait had the grace to obtain and consume it in his chapel at Lambeth. Pelham Dale, a Cambridge Don, was arrested and Mr. Green was kept over a year in durance vile. John Bright in the Liberal Cabinet pleaded for Mr. Green when he found he was imprisoned in the same Castle as Fox, the founder of the Quakers. John Bull began to feel uneasy and popular opinion veered against the persecution. The Church Association ceased attempting imprisonments and Mr. Martin withdrew after fifteen years' litigation against Father Mackonochie. Archbishop Tait felt unhappy on his deathbed and requested Green's release and Mackonochie's exchange of benefice. Mackonochie accordingly left St. Alban's and wandering later upon the Scotch hills perished in the snow. There, no doubt, had the finger of God touched him. He became a hero and a saint enshrined unto the High Church.

Archbishop Tait died leaving the Ritualists irresistible. Throughout his life he was a stern but diplomatic opponent to the Oxford Movement. He had been at Balliol with Manning and Ward. He always set his Anglican ideal above the fortunes of his friends. He dropped Ward and Newman after Tract 90, and later Temple and Jowett over the *Essays and Reviews*. He kept the Church statesmanlike and the State Anglican. He held the balance by leaning towards Dissent and eschewing Rome. When the High Church rose in horror at the sacrilegious Communion given in the Abbey to a Unitarian Bible Reviser, Tait laid down that doctrine of "occasional Conformity," which had been so fiercely debated under Queen Anne. He took the line of least or lowest resistance. He would not back Wilberforce's protest against the Vatican Council exclusion of Anglicans nor bless the two Bishops who attended the Old Catholic Conference afterwards. He was willing to shelve the Athanasian Creed, and bury Dissenters in Church ground. These were two very bitter points with the High Church, who if not able to dispose of the souls of Dissenters, felt they had some say about their bodies. They fought the Burials Act under Salisbury and Hope, but in vain, for the country accepted and passed it as a sanitary measure! Cautious and canny, Tait was not without a certain measure of majesty. Because he was a compromiser, his name is forgotten, but his Primacy was the ablest of his century.

Samuel Wilberforce was the one great Anglican Prelate

that the Oxford Movement bred. Although he held un-flinching views about Rome and Ritualism, he wielded the balance of Parties. If Pusey kept the rope tight, Wilberforce walked it. However much he openly resisted, he secretly rode the Movement. His *Life* disclosed nauseated horror when daughter or brother seceded to Rome, but the letters which passed between him and Robert are the most moving recorded in the whole Movement. Never was fraternal agony deeper than in their parting. Once Samuel had settled for himself as an Anglican that God had preserved "to us alone so completely the Catholic element," he never looked aside or back. He was the leader and fighter on the Bishop's Bench, but he threatened Robert to resign his own Bishopric. In vain he cast him Andrewes, Cosin, Hooker, and Bramhall as Anglican lifebuoys. He analysed the causes of disintegration in his brother's mind: the power originally assumed by Newman, Manning's "subtlety of intellect" working against Robert's humility, "whilst your late unhappy Archbishop of York has been exhibiting the Church of England as few but he could exhibit it." It was in vain but it was a noble and a piercing letter. There must have been many such written in those tragic days.

Wilberforce brought the Essayists before Convocation and obtained a pronouncement on Doctrine for the first time since 1711. He led the discussion against Colenso and so hot was the fight amongst the Bishops that at one moment a venerable prelate moved that the Archbishops do now say prayers! He wrestled with the State in the person of Lord Chancellor Westbury, who made fun of his nickname and spoke of his "saponaceous" sentences in the House of Lords. Sam castigated him fairly, but he was less successful in his famous duel with Huxley, whom he challenged at Oxford on the Darwinian thesis. Wilberforce made the unforgivable mistake of asking Huxley whether he was descended from the ape on his grandfather's or grandmother's side! In spite of a packed audience of women and clergy Huxley's pulverising reply finished all episcopal interference in future scientific meetings.

Religion and Science used to clash in full and pounding panoply before the days when Scientists find excuses for a God-made Universe, and Anglican Theologians assert the dogmas of science as cheerfully as their own. Wilberforce, prompted by Professor Owen, attacked Darwin's "Origin of Species" in the *Quarterly*. By one of those accidents which are more comic than fiction the same Number preserved an article on "The Missing Link," which was no semi-human ape but the more angelic Deaconess, whom some Anglican writer was anxious to place between Curate and District Visitor.

Huxley's discomfiture of Wilberforce led Gladstone later to essay controversy on the destruction of the Gadarene swine on rather trivial lines. Was it a criminal act or not? If Gadara was Roman territory, it was immoral to destroy property; but if Gadara was under Jewish law, it would have been illegal for the proprietor to own them. This summarises a debate which is omitted from the *Life* of Gladstone, as possibly the Biographer was on the side of Huxley.

Anglicans and Romans were too busy holding the fort

HENRY EDWARD CARDINAL MANNING

against each other to meet the advance of Science, but the Catholics produced St. George Mivart, who with Samuel Butler was the only critic, whose criticisms kept Darwin awake at night. Lord Acton recorded that Mivart was black-balled at the *Athenæum* by intolerant Darwinians. Mivart was admirable in writing his *Genesis of Species* or his monograph on the Cat, but when he began to write on *Happiness in Hell* there was trouble. In a fit of irritability caused by disease, he later apostatised and was offered a triumphant banquet by the Darwinians. This he was unable to attend as he died earlier on the same day. Cardinal Vaughan would not allow him Catholic burial, but from his deathbed extended the benefit of the doubt or the benefit of the Faith, whichever way we regard it. The condition was accepted under the Cardinal's successor and the body of Mivart was translated to holy ground. A pleasant victory of medical charity over strictly interpreted Canon Law.

Whichever way the law decided questions of ritual, the law was generally disobeyed. Englishmen cannot be made Catholics or Protestants by legal decisions. Force naturally has always worked inversely. Queen Mary assured the Reformation and Queen Elizabeth hardened the Catholics into a Papal Party, each by the simple process of providing martyrs. The Ritualists had confessors under Victoria when clergymen were sent to prison under the Public Worship Regulation Bill. But the time had passed when the trend of the Movement or even the fortunes of the Church could be altered by Act of Parliament or private prejudice of the Prime Minister.

Gladstone wrested from Disraeli the coveted power of making Bishops in the spirit of recovering Holy Ground from an unbeliever. It has been an Anglican feature for Bishops to be coloured by the Prime Minister's opinions. Disraeli was eclectic or election-wise, for he sent the Erastian Tait to Canterbury, the High Church Benson to Truro, and the Protestant Ryle to Liverpool. He never forgot that he enjoyed the worldly advantages of Anglican baptism, but he had lost his enthusiasm for Young Englanders who alone could have fulfilled his early dreams. The High Church had great innings with Gladstone and Salisbury as Premiers. Gladstone appointed High Church Bishops, because he thought they were right, and Salisbury, because he thought the Low Church were wrong. The Sovereign still interfered at times. Queen Victoria declined High Churchmen for her Household, prevented Liddon becoming a Bishop, and promoted the future Archbishop Davidson against Salisbury's approval. King Edward in later days wished to assert himself as "Defender of the Faith" against putting a Modernist into a See. The experiment of making Modernists into Bishops has always succeeded in England. Temple, one of the abused Essayists and Reviewers, became orthodox enough to crown King Edward. Every effort had once been made to acquaint Edward with the mild German theology of the Prince Consort, but there were too many cooks stirring the broth. Even at his Baptism apocrypha tell that the rite had to be repeated because one Archbishop said the words and the other splashed the water, whereas valid Baptism requires that they should be performed by the same person. Cardinal Vaughan vouched for the repetition of his Baptism by the Chaplain of the Queen of the Belgians.

Meantime, to soothe the Queen, Tait introduced the Bill, which Disraeli elegantly described as a means for putting down "the Mass in Masquerade." Gladstone immediately challenged and the Oxford Movement was transferred to a grand debate in the House. There was a division of consciences. Liberals would not follow Gladstone in his pontifical Resolutions. On the other hand, High Church Tories so resented Disraeli's bitterness that they opposed him later in his Eastern Policy. The Bill was a temporary triumph for Disraeli, the Queen, and the Low Church. A few parsons went to prison as previously described and all went on as before.

It was twenty-four years after this Bill and a month after Gladstone's death, before Ritual was debated again by the Commons. Harcourt, who had seceded from Gladstone on the first occasion, now led the Protestant attack on the Oxford Movement. He was what Disraeli called "a Parliamentary Christian" and accused Lord Halifax of conducting a Conspiracy to bring the Church of England into reunion with Rome. As President of the English Church Union, Halifax had become a lay pontiff more influential than any Bishop. From the Bishops' Bench, Creighton of London mocked Harcourt as a new Elijah demanding that someone should slay the priests of Baal. In the Commons, Lord Salisbury's son and nephew, Lord Hugh Cecil and Mr. Balfour, defended the High Church in the best Oxford style. There was no result and ten years passed before another Commission had completed the labours of examining the practices of the Church. It was clear that the High Church with their sacred points, Vestments, Eastward Position, Lights, Mixed Chalices, and other Roman ceremonial, were winning all down the line.

It was noticeable that the conflict was fiercer on matters of Ritual than over such a sheet anchor as Divorce. The Church of England faithfully reflects public opinion, and her attitude discloses that John Bull dislikes Ritual but accepts Divorce. Divorce does not entail exclusion from his Church. His Creed could be summarised as belief in two Sacraments necessary and two wives permissible unto salvation. Rome by insisting on Seven Sacraments and one wife appears to him extravagant in modern times. Rome has naturally opposed Divorce in England as everywhere, but the safeguard of the annulment has been the cause of deep and prolonged controversy in the English Press, arising from the Marconi and Marlborough cases. Since the question of Anglican Orders no Roman decision has been more thoroughly bolted to the bran. The Church of England admits certain nullity cases and has officially fought Divorce, but there have been temporisings in her attitude. The Savoy Chapel could defy Bishops and give divorcees a marriage service. Even Bishop King allowed the innocent to remarry. Archbishop Maclagen of York fought his own Chancellor for issuing licenses to the guilty parties.

Riots, lawsuits, and persecution all failed. Ritual spread and spread until it reached the Bishop's Bench. Bishop

King of Lincoln was the first to assume mitre and vestments and in consequence steps were at once taken, to
bring him to trial. Archbishop Benson was directed to
proceed by the Chancellor, though he took the safe line
of neither denying nor assuming jurisdiction. He backed
himself with five Bishops. John Bull has been fair enough
in religious persecution. He is responsible for both Protestant and Catholic martyrs in the past. In 1841 Holy-
oake was sent to prison for atheism and fifty years later
the Bishop of Lincoln was tried and condemned on such
criminal charges as making the Sign of the Cross with
upraised hand, mixing the Chalice "and afterwards drinking such water and wine before the congregation." The
Bishop won on the Eastward Position, singing the *Agnus
Dei,* and lighted candles. The angry Protestants appealed
to the Privy Council, who found with some common sense
that the Bishop had no responsibility for candles he had
not lighted himself! It was a victory for toleration.

As an example of the prevailing tolerance, Archbishop
Tait died under a sense of mistaken zeal and Archbishop
Benson turned the Lincoln Trial in favour of high Ritual
once and for all. As A. M. Fairbairn, the Nonconformist
writer of *Catholicism Roman and Anglican,* summarised:
"In 1833 the first issue of the Tracts began breathing the
courage, defiance and furious despair of a forlorn hope.
In 1890 the men, who have replaced the old leaders, are
within the Citadel victorious proposing their own terms."

The Lincoln Judgment reversed all previous Judgments
and opened the flood gates to Ritual. It was oddly reckoned "the severest blow the Church of England had re-

ceived since the glorious Reformation!" The triumphs of the High Church have since been overwhelming. Vestments have appeared even in Cathedrals such as Lichfield, Rochester, and Truro. In St. Paul's Cathedral the Church Association made a despairing attack on the reredos as idolatrous, but were quashed by Bishop Temple's veto. John Bull then learnt of a reredos as "a thing to put peoples' backs up!"

In 1899 the Bishops petitioned the Archbishops about Incense and Processional Lights. The answer was that they were permissible by the Crown: in other words, Ritual could be extended by the Home Secretary in the same way as drinking during illegal hours. It was a pious opinion of the Archbishops, and those, who held the equally pious opinion that incense was Biblical, went their way. Later the Bishops sought a permissive use of Vestments on grounds of reverence and seemly order, but not for sacramental reasons. Primitive vestments were secular raiment used for seemly order at the Christian Mysteries until they became sacred and hieratic. It seemed the wish of the Bishops to restore them to their origins and permit them on grounds that would apply equally to a Mayor's robe or a Verger's gown. If there are threads to be unstitched from the Anglican web they appear to be not only Compromise but Common Sense and Tolerance. Reasons will be found for tolerating even what is irrational. The broad comprehension both of taste and belief appears in a pleasant letter of Green the historian describing his Curates: "One is a Catholic. He breakfasts at 12.30 in a cassock and biretta. The second is an Anglican who spends his day organising petitions to the Lord Primate. The third is a musician who sets the general Confession to operatic music. The fourth is a literateur who reads Balzac all the week." This no doubt is symbolic of the Church of England at her leisured best.

The success of the Ritualists led to Harcourt's pompous campaign in the House of Commons and to Lady Wimborne's agitation through the National Church League. Harcourt posed as the last great Protestant and Lady Wimborne (whose nephew, the Duke of Marlborough, later became a Catholic) led the dispirited Low Church like a Victorian Joan of Arc. The agitation led to a final Commission of Ritual, which reported in 1906 establishing the statistics and influence of the High Church. Out of 14,000 Benefices over 5,000 were found tainted by some illegality. Only a dozen were left Protestant enough to be deficient in the ritual demanded by the Prayer Book. But the majority of the witnesses were hirelings of the Protestant underworld.

The crux and pith of the Oxford Movement ran to the question whether Anglican Orders were valid, whether the Clergy were properly ordained in the ancient manner so that a Greek Catholic or a Russian Orthodox could attend Anglican service and a Roman Catholic dying beyond reach of his priests, need not hesitate to ask for the Last Sacraments and Absolution from the nearest Parson. Did every clergyman possess *in posse,* whether he knew it or not, the potential powers of a Roman Priest? Were the jovial Latitudinarians, or sincere Nonjuring Bishops the lineal successors of the Apostles and of the mediæval founders of English Sees?

There had always been men with Gallican leanings, like Lingard, who had believed in Anglican Orders, even as a pious improbability. Converts like Pugin and De Lisle clung to the belief that their former mother was an honest woman. Rome always re-ordained convert parsons, but there appeared to be no decision from the Pope. A combination of strong individual characters brought this about in 1896; the tolerant benevolence of the aging Pope Leo, the unquenchable enthusiasm of Lord Halifax, the Gallican scholarship of such French clerics as Portal and Duchesne, and the determined vigilance of Cardinal Vaughan. For a year an Anglo-Roman Review buzzed merrily between the Churches. Archbishop Benson was for wise dissuasion but Lord Halifax overwhelmed him by telegraphing joyous news and arriving with Portal and messages from Rome uninvitedly. Portal had talked boldly to the Pope, who wished to make his *Nunc Dimittis* in favour of the Anglicans. Halifax addressed Benson as *alterius orbis papa* but threatened him with the tier in Hell reserved for those who lose great opportunities. Benson, who disapproved of the very existence of Roman Catholics in England, remained doubtful. Their Church he had described as "the uncatholic and unchristian act of sending an Italian Mission to attack this ancient Church." But Halifax had warmed the Pope's heart and Leo wrote a letter *ad Anglos* (not *ad Anglicanos*). In his innocence His Holiness unfortunately referred to Indulgences and recommended prayers to the Virgin. England received it with the respect due to a very old and harmless man. His next step was to call a Commission of prelates in Rome, including two famous future Cardinals, Gasparri and

Merry del Val, who though happy in an English mother
had no desire for an Anglican one. The aged Mr. Gladstone forwarded a memorandum which was given to
Cardinal Rampolla, and the mills of Rome began to
grind very slowly. Cardinal Mazzella presided with im-
partiality, and enthusiasts watched with intense curiosity
for the result. Three Englishmen had come out from
Cardinal Vaughan not merely to scotch but to kill anglican Orders: Abbot Gasquet, Mgr. Moyes, and the Franciscan Provincial Fleming. Three foreigners, Duchesne,
Gasparri, and a Jesuit, opposed them, while two Anglicans, Canon Lacey and a Cowley Father, waited in the
offing to give information. These two gentlemen produced a persuasive document in faultless Latin *de Re Anglicana,* which impressed the Cardinals, but the weight
of historic evidence had gone against even the hopeful-
ness of the Pope. Abbot Gasquet found a copy of the Bull
Praeclara carissimi, by which Paul IV had directed that
priests ordained under King Edward VI must be re-
ordained under Queen Mary. Every copy of this Bull had
disappeared in England. The Commission fought out
every point. The name of Barlow was bruited in Rome.
Even telegrams and despatches passed concerning the
long-forgotten Barlow. The astutest thought in two
Churches was concentrated on this obscure Bishop of the
past.

And the old queries arose:

Was Barlow a Bishop?

Did he intend to consecrate Parker a Catholic Bishop?

Had Cranmer's interference with the wording of the
Ordinal left it possible for him to do so?

These were the questions which the Roman Commission was debating. Had the defect ever been re-supplied by a real Catholic Bishop? What were the precedents on either side? It was found that the Catholic Archbishop of Spoleto had assisted at the Consecration of the Anglican Bishop Fenton in 1617. But it was Archbishop Abbot who said the all-important words. It was discovered that in 1704 the Anglican Bishop Gordon of Galloway had submitted to Rome and had been re-ordained.

It was the same with Bishop Casey, who was made Bishop of Limerick under Edward VI, and who was reconciled to Rome as a Priest but not as a Bishop. Cardinal Pole had not re-ordained the Priests ordained during the Schism of Henry, but only those ordained during the Heresy of Edward. As for Archbishop Parker's consecration, Scory and Coverdale, who assisted Barlow as Edwardian Bishops, had fled the country under Mary. But Barlow and Hodgkin, the latter certainly, had been consecrated by the Sarum Ordinal. They all laid their hands on Archbishop Parker. Were the assistants also consecrators? What was their intention and what was the form of their Ordinal? The old Sarum Ordinal said:

"Receive authority to offer sacrifices to God and to celebrate Masses as well for the quick as the dead."

The new Anglican Ordinal said:

"Take thou authority to preach the Word of God and to minister the Holy Sacraments."

There was obviously an essential difference in wording and intention. The new Ordinal might have applied to Presbyterians. In fact the Church of England recognized Presbyterian Orders between the years 1552 and 1662, when the last chance of reunion was dissipated by the Savoy Conference.

The Roman Commission had to make a decision and they compared the Edwardine Prayer Book with the old Missal. In sixteen places the mentions of sacrifice were cut out. The kernel was missing, so the nut was not so hard to crack. Pope Leo had been reported impartial. He had been told with equal authority that the recognition or condemnation of Anglican Orders would bring a large secession to Rome. He may have been willing to recognise them but the evidence gave him no chance. Abbot Gasquet and the Provincial Fleming were responsible for the Bull *Apostolicae Curae,* which described the Orders of the Anglican Church as null and invalid. It was pronounced by the Pope "with great solemnity and probably with regret." Nevertheless as Father Tyrrell wrote to Lord Halifax: "if Rome were to eat her words she would soon cease to be worth uniting with."

Archbishop Benson died dramatically before the answer of the Anglican Archbishops was signed and Archbishop Temple took up his pen. They hailed Rome as a sister-Church and the Pope as a venerable brother. They congratulated him on abandoning as an essential what was called the Porrection of the Instruments, the delivery of the Mass vessels to the newly ordained. They pointed out the great uncertainty under Cardinal Pole. Some of the Edwardian priests had been involuntarily re-ordained, but they had been deprived for wedlock not for defect of Order: as invalid husbands not invalid clergymen. The Archbishops claimed that the Roman rite of Confirmation was defective and that the Church of England went back in the Sixteenth Century to the Roman starting point almost. The original rite was austere but the Romans had adorned it with Gallican embellishments. The whole controversy passed into details of history and liturgy.

Rome had used both the historic and dogmatic argument. Historically it has been Rome's consistent policy from the days of Cardinal Pole to re-ordain *absolutely*, not conditionally, all those who had received Orders according to the Edwardian ritual. This important historic fact the Church could prove to evidence. Dogmatically, the basic argument was the defect of intention and the exclusion of the Catholic concept of the Sacrifice and the Priesthood, as these were contained in the Sarum and other ancient rituals and were wholly lacking in the new Ordinals.

The Pope's Bull left the Churches as they were but in more defined camps. The huge majority of Anglican Clergy did not care or perhaps understand. Many were definitely annoyed and a very few came over on antiquarian lines to Rome. Mgr. Barnes a quarter of a century later restated the astounding possibility that Barlow was neither valid nor invalid. He may never have been any Bishop at all! The supposition depended on detective work. The Diocesan Registers of the Canterbury Province are perfect in every See save those connected with Barlow (St. Asaph, St. David, and Bath and Wells). The Chapter Records for the same three are missing for Barlow's years. Were the documents destroyed or hidden? Was it to prevent their proving Barlow was or was not a Bishop, for their disappearance cuts both ways?

The sensible Anglican knows he can no longer rest his Orders on such a reed as Barlow. Nor does he rely on history or theology but on Providence to make good the defect and endorse them by Grace, though Newman points out that this must hold good equally for Dissenters. The Greek Church declared the Pope's Bull erroneous, but could not enter into Communion with the Anglican Church until Doctrine was adjusted.

If the Pope had recognised Anglican Orders, there would have been singular confusion. Convert clergy would have ceased to join the Roman Rite, for the bulk of the High Church would have claimed to keep their English Rite and English wives as a Uniate Church. England would have shared the ecclesiastical crazy quilt of the East. The faithful would have been distracted between Roman Catholics, Anglican Uniates in communion with Rome, Anglo-Catholics in communion with Canterbury.

The term "null and void" was naturally irritating to the Anglican clergy. It means in practise that for Dean Inge to give Cardinal Bourne Absolution on his deathbed would be *null* in the eyes of Rome and likewise for Bishop Barnes of Birmingham to celebrate at a Eucharistic Congress would be deemed a *void* ceremony.

The question of Anglican Orders is technically regarded as a *factum theologicum dogmaticum,* a fact intimately connected with revelation. Catholic theologians agree that Anglican Orders are certainly invalid and that they have been declared such by the Bull of Leo XIII. For Catholics the matter is therefore settled.

Obviously, it does not touch in any way the fact that

Nonjurors who may have obtained and passed on valid Orders from a Greek or Jansenist Bishop are truly possessed of Catholic Orders. Even today, if any High Anglican group had courage to have a few valid Bishops ordained in the East, they could prove a thorn to the State and a puzzle to the Roman Hierarchy. What Rome would do is a matter of misty futurity, but it is not likely that the lines between Rome and Canterbury will remain exactly the same for another hundred years, or that Reunion will not have been attempted before three more centuries have passed.

IV

THE PRESENT PHASE

The third phase of the Oxford Movement came to an end in 1896 with the Bull *Apostolicae Curae*. It was also marked by the death of Archbishop Benson, the first High Church Primate. He was succeeded by Temple, who having been persecuted as a Modernist had no will to push even extremists to the wall. Benson had been an anti-Roman Ritualist. The streak of genius in his wife's character was shown in his children, of whom one became the celebrated convert Monsignor Benson.

Such filial reactions were a feature of English religious life. There is a list of Anglican Bishops whose sons have become reconciled with Rome, from Cosin of Durham and Toby Mathew of York to Thorold of Rochester, and Knox of Manchester. In another field, Lord Shaftesbury's grandson became President of the Ritualists. On the other hand, Beresford Hope's son could not hear of Church matters without profanity, according to the *Book of the Beresford Hopes*. The entire Oxford Movement had been a reaction against *lax latitudinarianism*. The English nature is such that it reacts equally from the chill or from the hothouse, as Catholic educationalists have discovered in the Schools of Religious Orders. Whereas souls suffering from religious anæmia found Rome a remedy, Catholics seldom found relief in Anglicanism. A full history of the Movement should provide counter-lists of converts and reverts.

With 1896 the lines had become defined between the Churches, and conversions were the order of the day. Two volumes appeared: *Roads to Rome* and its feeble step-sister *Roads from Rome.* The names included in the former were distinguished and familiar enough. The latter included two Redemptorists and an Oratorian. Most archivists of Religious Orders in England could probably have provided a more formidable contrast. A third list could be made of those who have verted more than twice.

With the new century the siren on the horizon for both Churches assumed the voice of Modernism. Roman and Anglican had both realised that the Church which could best meet, inveigle, or explain Science would win a large public which was drifting away from all Churches. Evangelicals had treated Science as the Devil escaping from the test-tube, but the Broad Church over-hastily accepted every finding of Science on their knees. An interesting attempt had been made by Bishop Gore to bridge the gulf between the Incarnation and Evolution. Under his editorship appeared *Lux Mundi,* whereupon the old Tractarians found the Scriptures moving under them. The young High Churchmen were trying to make a compact between theories as different as the Binomial Theorem and the day of the week Thursday. The Incarnation is miracle and revelation of faith. Evolution is theory and experiment, applied in another mode and on a different plane. Its residuum of proved facts is small, to say the least, and with that Rome would never quarrel. The rest, where not proved false, remains uncertain. A hundred dimensions separate the two most remotely different ideas that have ever entered into the mind of man. But the Oxford School held that both were true and so could be reconciled. *Lux Mundi* was their gallant effort. It resembled a desire to include Angles in a handbook of Zoölogy. Under Archbishop Temple both Modernists and Ritualists ran ahead. In the Roman Church there is no sphere for improvement in ritual such as Anglicanism presented, but Modernism was bound to offer a fallacious philosophical attraction to subtle and unstable minds. Ritual controversy has always been stupid and local, but the Modernist movement, which burst on the Catholic Church, became historical and of serious consequence. Indirectly it was connected also with the Oxford Movement. The writings of Newman, unlike those of Aquinas, were liable to exquisite misinterpretation and from them Father Tyrrell mistakenly developed his head-strong course, while Christendom watched admiringly first, before the true nature of the movement had been disclosed, but finally aghast. Modernism, as it proved, was the shadow not the light falling from Newman.

Modernism has its own history, of which Father Tyrrell found himself, to his grim pleasure, the figure-head and sometimes the target. Deeply as he had been influenced by Newman, it is only fair to remark that he left his teacher far behind. He hailed the spirit of Newman, apart from his system, as an imperishable acquisition, but he wrote: "I feel Newman cannot help us any more. It is not the Articles of the Creed but the word *Credo* that needs adjustment." He vaguely described Modernism as the reconciliation of what the Saints have lived on with Modern Knowledge. Pius X preferred to regard it as a compendium of heresies and congratulated Dr. Dwyer, Bishop of Limerick, for disentangling Newman from Modernism in a pamphlet.

Tyrrell was not an Oxford man but he attempted to give Rome what the School of *Lux Mundi* had given the Anglicans. In his troubles he drew the sympathy of Anglicans who have always turned hopefully towards a falling man, every tremor of Rome appearing to add to Anglican stability. They looked to Tyrrell as they once looked to Döllinger and Loisy, but Tyrrell preferred to perish between the Churches. His influence which Rome rejected, returned to the Church of his baptism. Modernism found its way into the High Church group apart from the Broad Church, which has attained all lengths consistent with any belief at all. What is more important and more interesting, within the Anglican Church, the Oxford Movement has stooped to give Modernism a lift. This has given Modernism a currency which Rome denied it, for the Church of England still spreads the doctrines of the Oxford Movement over wide portions of the world. Pan-Anglicanism showed itself in 250 Bishops at the Lambeth Conference. The idle words of W. S. Gilbert in the *Bab Ballads* were fulfilled:

> "From East and South the holy clan
> Of Bishops gathered to a man
> To Synod called Pan-Anglican."

Bishop Gore was not present at the 1920 Conference, preferring to preside over the Anglo-Catholic Congress. In the last ten years before his death he outweighed all the Bishops in personal influence and erudition. In spite of his tinge of Modernism he succeeded to Pusey and left no successor. As a controversialist his *Roman Catholic Claims* must be studied with Dom Chapman's reply, the last exchange of learned polemics in the old manner. His editorship of *Lux Mundi* proved a *Crux Ecclesiae* for it installed the new thought. Scripture was accepted as inspired but not accurate. An Anglo-Catholic restatement of his doctrine appeared in *Essays Catholic and Critical,* which left miracles an open question.

Gore and Tyrrell, as thinkers, both strove to reconcile new vintage with venerable bottles. Gore attacked Rome historically but made every advance possible in theology. Tyrrell was the reverse, clinging to the Rome of history but undermining her very theology. Their fates were largely a result of temperament. Gore passed from See to See to die in honourable retirement as general consultant to the High Church. The Irish Jesuit went out into the wilderness forever.

George Tyrrell was an Anglo-Irish convert whom the Jesuits had trained to clear preaching and exquisite writing. Paradox and persiflage gave him the clever feeling that he could juggle with dogmas. He first criticised not Catholicism but the manner in which theologians presented it. He criticised Theology for deducing stern prose from poetical premises. He distinguished between the collective mind of all the faithful and the Governing Power of the Church. But the faithful could not come to his support and the Governing Power was bound to discipline him. The truth was that like Mivart he was affected by incurable bodily disease and could not help being goaded or resist goading others. Sensible thoughts that sensible people keep to themselves he flung into rude words. His "much abused letter" to a professor in doubt appeared ill-translated in Italian and brought the Church roof on his head. Though he defended it to his General as "medicine in extreme cases," the Jesuits reluctantly let him go. After he had answered the Pope's Bull on Modernism in the *Times* he was excommunicated. Modernists were thrown into dismay and for a long time more than normal caution was employed. Weaker thinkers left the Church, but many like Baron von Hugel remained under the cloaks of submission or mysticism. Humility proved an escape from ecclesiastical penalties which Tyrrell's exasperated temperament refused to speak. It was once again the contrast of an Acton and a Döllinger. One was taken and one was left.

To return to the Church of England, Archbishop Temple died soon after he had crowned the new King. The Victorian interference with the Church was over. The old Queen had looked on the Church of England as her Church in the sense that she spoke of "her Navy" or "her Army." She turned the impressionable Disraeli into her Protestant. She prevented great High Churchmen becoming Bishops. Tait possessed her two requirements for an Archbishop. He was subservient and Presbyterian. She accepted Benson who was Gladstone's High Church candidate. Benson was not subservient, as he declined her wish not to oppose the Deceased Wife's Sister Bill. But it is curious to find a certain Mr. Davidson, Tait's son-in-law, persuading the Queen to accept Benson, especially on account of "personal devotion to Your Majesty." Davidson had Tait's qualities and the Queen made him Dean of Windsor and Primate *in petto*.

In fullness of time Davidson succeeded Temple. He was ironically described as a very good man without principles, in other words a perfect Anglican Bishop, for he carried compromise to a fine art. There was nothing on which he would not make reservation except the Sacrament. His platitudinous pliancy became the strength as well as the weakness of his Communion during the quarter of a century that he ruled. He became a better and better Primate while his principles became softer and softer, until he was suggesting reunion with Presbyterians on the one hand and patronising Bishop Gore's conversations with Cardinal Mercier on the other. Rome would prefer the reverse type in history, even a bad man like the Borgias, provided he kept strong principles.

There are three refuges open to Anglican isolation: the Dissenters, Rome, and Greece. It is possible for a good Anglican to shake hands with all three but it is impossible to embrace more than one at a time.

A celebrated attempt was made in 1913 on the African mission fields to unite Low Church Anglicans with Dissenters in one Communion. Bishop Weston of Zanzibar cried Heresy very loudly and returned to make appeal to Lambeth. The Primate gave a very equivocal judgment, but the High Church had found a strenuous and mediæval leader in Bishop Weston, in whom charity, logic, and invincible enthusiasm were united with conflict. The controversy was associated with the name of Kikuyu and was allowed to simmer out in the Dark Continent. The Anglican Bishops at home had already burnt their fingers in Africa.

The approach to the Greek Church has led to a friendly shake across not a gulf but over the bulky impediment of the Latin Church. Rome is halfway to Constantinople not *vice versa.*

When you have broken with your canonical wife, it does not mend matters to flirt with your mother-in-law, however venerable. As far as helping the Reunion of Christendom, it is like building a top story before securing the basement. As Pobedonesteff wrote from the Holy Synod to the Anglicans, the difficulty was "because you came out of Rome and she remains in the history both of your Church and of your people." Since old Dr. Routh requested the Russian Bishops to admit an Anglican to Communion, reconciliation rather than recognition has been achieved. Bishop Creighton of London attended the Coronation of the last Czar, clad in his pontificals. All that was friendly and diplomatic was continually done, but the Prayer Book remains far more a Roman than a Byzantine document.

Bishop Wordsworth of Salisbury made advances to the Swedish and Moravian Churches. The Old Catholic sect of Jansenists declined his challenge to recognise Anglican Orders, but they have since come to terms and their Bish-

ops have assisted in the consecration of Anglican Bishops
and received Communion in St. Paul's. This is a great
change-over since 1894, when Wordsworth remonstrated
with the Archbishop of Utrecht and the Old Catholics
replied quoting Macaulay that under Elizabeth unor-
dained people had been admitted to serve the Sacraments. The Anglicans now enjoy a spiritual Treaty of
Utrecht.

The Reunion policy issued by Lambeth since the War
has been perfectly fair and even courageous. The Conference invited the re-ordination of others but were willing
to accept re-ordination themselves. On these lines Christendom could be reunited faster than any Geneva Conference could disarm Europe. The acid test lies in the
question, Would Anglicans, who impose Orders on Dissenters, be willing to receive unconditional Roman ones?
T. S. Eliot writes of Dissenters accepting Bishops "as a
harmless formality for the sake of a phantom unity." But
Roman re-ordination would be neither formality in Catholic, nor harmless in Protestant, eyes.

The much dreaded Deceased Wife's Sister Bill was
passed under King Edward, after which canonical offend-
ers could be received at Court and presumably at Lambeth. To Rome it was only a question of dispensation, but
the State had changed the terms of Communion in the
State Church. Davidson was equal to the occasion. He ad-
vised his clergy neither to marry Deceased Wife's Sisters
in church nor refuse them Communion. In other words,
they were refused a minor but permitted a major Sacrament. Davidson played the game of Reunion fairly and

smoothly, knowing in his heart that it would remain an impossibility in his time. Reunion with Dissent meant conditions which dissolved any hopes from Rome. Reunion with Constantinople meant accepting terms which would keep Dissenters from rejoining their mother Church. Yet progress was made in two directions, for a Greek Patriarch was found willing to admit Anglican Orders and at Malines a Catholic group, acting in a purely private capacity and unrecognised by Rome, met Anglican delegates. The two parties, headed respectively by Cardinal Mercier and Bishop Gore, found themselves at one on the Eucharist. Davidson trusted to his common sense that Malines would fail or he would not have extended his nervous patronage. The suggested possibilities were interesting: such as Papal Supremacy acting through the English Primate: Re-ordination of Anglican Priests: Retention of Mass in English: Communion in both kinds, and Clerical marriage for a generation. In the end it was found impossible to put the Anglican omelette back into the Roman eggshell. Optimists only hoped that Mercier and Gore could continue their conference in the next world.

The National Church Assembly was brought into existence after the War to relieve Parliament of Church business. It gave Home Rule to Anglicans but reserved a veto to the House of Commons. Malines stirred the sleeping Protestantism of the House and led to the defeat of the Revised Prayer Book. In vain the Assembly prepared and the Bishops backed this admirable facing-two-ways piece of liturgy. If it could be passed, an appeal could be made with added force to what was called "loyalty to the Prayer Book."

The difficulty had always been to be loyal to a book that was often not loyal to itself. The new book was loyal all round. It was a primer of comprehensives. The Anglo-Catholic found his Mass. The Modernist was spared the pain of enunciating pains in the future. The Evangelical could wander into extemporary prayer. The Anglican dead had the agreeable surprise of being prayed for. Hitherto the Church of England let the dead pray for the dead. Wakeman wrote that the Anglican clergy were never so united as under the reigns of George III and IV. The reign of George V found them never so disunited, but the New Prayer Book was a bid to enclose them in one fold. The Bishops hoped they could hold back the Ritual tide by legalising a standard of illegality. Davidson sat like Canute in St. Augustine's Chair almost believing the courtiers who bade him halt the Anglo-Catholic waves . . . thus far and no further.

Parliament was simply asked to pass "the Book of 1662 with additions and deviations approved in 1928." It seemed a guileless request. The Lords consented but the Commons broke into furious debate. That Protestant type of mind which is equally suspicious of mixed bathing and mixed chalices was roused to fury. Though the National Church wished to be labelled Catholic in service as well as Creed, the Commons held that the Nation was Protestant still. Members found consciences to obey and constituencies to please. A party described by Bishop Hensley

Henson as "illiterates led by octogenarians" came to the surface. The more the Commons looked into the Book, the more restive they became. Parliament was asked to legalise Vestments. The Pope appeared to stand at the door, for there was a choice of Communion or Mass. Of lesser import were alternative Lessons and a revised Calendar. The Calendar was the keynote of the venture: an attempt to assimilate British Nationalism with a gesture towards Rome. St. Valentine was dropped but King Alfred came in. Patrick, Cuthbert, Columba, and Aidan represented Celtic Christianity, while such flowers of Rome as Leo the Great, Catherine of Siena, Bernard, Basil, and Francis of Assisi entered on their feast days. The Revisers had not the courage to introduce Laud or Becket, two English Primates who had died rather than allow King or Parliament to master their Church. Indignant Protestants asked why Cranmer, Tyndall, and Wycliff were not admitted. It was a scholarly book, but neither Laud nor Becket would have died for it. The Anglo-Catholics had no spokesman while the Protestant Low Church rallied under Lord Brentford, a diminuendo and unaristocratic Lord Shaftesbury. The High Church plot was unveiled. Under the new wording of the Visitation of the Sick, Reservation of the Sacrament was discovered. The Black Rubric, which enjoined kneeling at the Communion but slighted the Real Presence, had been omitted. In the second and vain attempt to pass the Commons the Black Rubric was restored to placate black Protestants. Twice the Commons rejected the Book and much of Davidson's life work passed down the noisy Parliamentary spout.

Enough honest and blind prejudice came to the surface to show that episcopal diplomacy and liturgical duplicity were unacceptable in John Bull's official Guidebook to Heaven.

Only the English could have devised such a contradictory term as a "Black Rubric": and only in England would a Socialist leader like Lansbury appear as the defender of High Ritual. But Lansbury came from Poplar and in Poplar the famous Father Dolling ended his life after Davidson had driven him out of the Porstmouth slum, in which he practised Christian Socialism and High Mass. Father Dolling was unique, a rough-and-ready Vincent de Paul, whose memory has proved one of the glories and one of the stumblingblocks of the Church of England. The rule has always been when a Saint makes an appearance to worry him to death. All the targets attached by the Church Association were men of love and courage struggling in the slums: Fathers Lowder, Mackonochie, and Stanton. Dolling, with his Irish nature and superb indifference to comfort or promotion, proved the spark of genius which the Church of England needed to inflame direct and loving relations with poverty and Labour. Wherever Dolling worked, the Church of England scarcely knew herself. She became the Church of the English people, of the soldier and sailor, of the slum and the prostitute. Davidson had made Dolling resign on the score of saying Masses for the Dead. Dolling's work for the living might have excused his attentions to the dead. But Davidson disapproved of prayers for the Dead which he afterwards accepted in the revised Prayer Book. From the point of view of red tape he was serenely right and Dolling passed from slum to slum, while as Sidney Dark, the Archbishop's biographer, remarks, Davidson passed from palace to palace. Both were admirable men and Rome could be envious of both, but the work of Dolling was more eternal than the work of Archbishop Davidson.

One of the few advantages of living outside the Roman discipline has been the outcrop of eccentrics who have adorned Anglican life. Chance Biographies have spread the fame of Dolling and Hawker of Morwenstow. Hawker, the strangest and most gifted of them all, fell to the biographical talons of Baring Gould, who preserved an amusing stock of anecdote. He lived amongst the remnant of Cornish wreckers and smugglers, entering into their spirit and superstition. As a poet he surpassed Tennyson in his few lines on the Holy Graal and he wrote the anthem "Shall Trelawney Die?" His vestments in church were as strange as his vestures outside. He affected the Greek rite and used a cope for the Communion, but, because he was thought to resemble Cardinal Wiseman facially, he wore crimson gloves. On his deathbed he was unexpectedly received into Rome and a most violent controversy followed. Unknown to Baring Gould, he was already in touch with Catholics.

With Father Dolling account Charles Marson who in the Middle Ages would have been a Troubadour of Our Lady. His mocking letter still enlivens the heavy record of the last Ritual Commission. He used the Latin Rite. He defied Bishops. He gave up his bed to an old broken and diseased gypsy to die in. He filled in the form of the Char-

ity Organisation Society with the particulars of Our
Lord! Most famous of all was Father Stanton, for fifty
years Curate at St. Alban's, Holborn. Few men ever attained such love and power in London. He had shared
Father Mackonochie's troubles and was threatened again
in his old age, but there arose so mighty a protest from
his friends that Protestant valour took the discreeter part.
Simply because he was Father Stanton, Bishops and Parliament had to leave him alone.

Davidson was succeeded by Archbishop Long who
stepped into the Primatial buskins in time to open the
Lambeth Conference of 1930. Here the Anglo-Catholics
made their position clear as a bridge, not a ferry, between
Canterbury and Rome. The Conference strove to find the
old *via media* "between cricket and Christianity" and
made history by accepting Birth-control within Christian
limits. The questions of the future are not of dogma or
ritual. Ceremonies and symbols have been beaten into thin
dust by a century of dispute. Ritual cannot trouble the
Church of England again. The rocks ahead are more material. Church Tithes is a reef upon which she may be
jagged unless relieved by Disestablishment. Happy was
her Anglo-Irish sister to be rid of Tithes and the miserable duty of collecting them from the unwilling tiller of
the soil. Had the Irish Church known the day of her visitation, the hated Gladstone was her saviour, for he left
her richly endowed and free to revise her Prayer Book.
The Church of England may well pray to receive as full
a freedom and as rich a stirrup-cup on her way.

Nor is Doctrine likely to convulse the Church of Eng-

land again, for her only settled doctrine is that any doctrine may be held unofficially, whether it is the Primacy
of the Pope or the Creed of Eugenics. Her future may lie
with Modernism and certainly the future of Modernism
lies with her. Anglican Modernists at times make clear
and valuable additions to Thought if not to Theology. In
one case they have found a virulent champion. Since Dean
Swift no Churchman has shown such bitter courage as
Dean Inge. The two Deans would differ about Ireland,
but in facing matters of political or medical interest
neither would turn a page or a hair. Unbending intellectual scorn, polished literary form, a laughing pessimism, a
snug sounding-board, and a strong preference for God
arising chiefly from horror of Humanity make a powerful combination. Dean Inge lies across the track of the
Oxford Movement with a snarl. But he is the herald of
the Modernist future.

With the Disestablishment in the future the Oxford
Movement will reach its last stage. The immense power
and success of the Movement were vindicated at the Lambeth Conferences of 1920 and 1930. Whenever the High
Church produced a leader to rally round, his personal
influence outswung the whole Bishops' Bench. This was
shewn in Pusey, Lord Halifax, and Bishop Weston of
Zanzibar. Weston declared for a severance of the legal tie
as the price of liberty. Welsh Disestablishment was supported by Liberal Churchmen and the High Church have
always threatened their own Disestablishment as their last
ditch. For a century the Church has been retreating down
the steps of the Throne. It was a form of Disestablishment

to allow Jews and Catholics in Parliament, Dissenters to marry in Chapel or bury in Church ground. When it comes, it will only be the severing of the last thread which allows the Protestant State to impede and hinder a Catholic-minded Church. The Prime Minister will no longer be able to impose a Bishop like Barnes or a Dean like Inge.

Tithes may be dead weight dragging at the parson's neck but Modernism is a living question. Can the old skin hold the newest of wines? For that reason Bishop Barnes is the most significant element in Anglican thought. He is the reckless and lonely plougher of the wastes. Striding ahead in seven-league boots he has left the other Bishops behind like manikins in the public view. From the See once adorned by Bishop Gore he has hastened on his heedless experiment to find out whether Christian Churchmanship can be rid forever of miracle no less than of myth. Sometimes he stoops to puerile blasphemy. At other moments he scales the ladder of Science and seeks to push his vision into the stars.

Is it a sign of irony or insanity in a Bishop to issue the hopeless challenge to examine and compare the Consecrated Wafer under a microscope? Any schoolboy can tell him that there is no more difference to be found in the mere species alone than between Mr. Barnes and Bishop Barnes after his own consecration. For him the Sacraments are magic, and priestcraft a horrible deposit of the cavemen. He is at great pains to avoid being mistaken for a witch-doctor. He has wounded and worried Anglicans, but there is a certain meteoric glamour in a Bishop who imperils his soul (if he believes in one) in order to save (as he fondly imagines) his reason and the reason of his fellow-men. He has hunted Superstition as fiercely as Inquisitor ever hunted Heresy. For him Religion is limited in its forms but Science is infinite. The God of Infinity is apparent in mathematical terms and the Creed must be revised in scientific formulas. For him the Oxford Movement is dead and its adherents are only groping back to a stultified past. No voice can answer him from Birmingham unless it be from the cemetery of the Oratorians at Rednall where the author of that Movement lies and being dead yet speaketh.

APPENDIX

I. UNPUBLISHED POEM BY NEWMAN

The Bodleian Library preserves the original and un-printed poem which was written by Newman within a fortnight of his conversion, dated from his old College and sent to Mark Pattison, among whose papers it was found. It gives the impression that he had received a very cold welcome on returning from Littlemore to the haunts he had once dominated. It also supplies an interpretation of the angel-faces at the close of *Lead Kindly Light*. To his intense and sensitive nature they reflected his beloved friends.

THE CHANGED MOTHER*

So Oxford, once thy dear old towers
   Again today I see,
Each time looks like the last, tho' oft
   I yet may visit thee.

---

*The verses by Newman, here published for the first time, while containing some beautiful passages, will not enhance his literary reputation. They evidently were written in haste, at a moment of keen interior trial, and so were despatched to Pattison without further revision. But they are historically valuable and bring us into intimate contact with the soul of Newman at a period following almost immediately upon his conversion and at a supreme instant in his life. They strongly bring home to us the heroism of his act and the steadfastness of his faith. — *The Editor.*

But thou art changed, my Mother dear,
   On me why look'st thou so?
I scarce did think thy ancient smile
   Could clouded be with woe.

I scarce did think the time would come,
   When I should talk of you,
As of some town I once had seen
   But cared no more to view.

Am I, then, changed, or is it thou?
   Friends are not as we parted —
False friends look cold, tho' friends of youth,
   True friends, look broken-hearted.

Yes, friends of youth long, long ago —
   Whence sixteen lightsome summers
Had scarce passed o'er our careless heads —
   It well may overcome us.

Boyhood, youth, manhood! what a dream
   Of memory is expanding —
Year after year, thou, solemn guide
   Me to the grave wast handing!

What studious nights, what gatherings gay,
   What careless prayers or burning —
What journeys long, what journeys short,
   What deeds deep penance earning!

What words I heard, what words I said,
  Throughout the long years nine —
What sinners knew, what holy men —
  How vast a reckoning mine!

What shall I do, or whither go?
  There was one who did guide me —
But thou, changed Mother, tho' still dear,
  Hast frowned him from beside me.

Changed Mother! brethren yet I have,
  Beloved like my own brother —
But those my angels sweet, will go —
  Of them too thou art Mother.

Goodbye! changed Mother, oh goodbye!
  We part not in unkindness:
I half began these silly words
  In anger — 'twas my blindness.

I know that there are Saints in heaven
  And Christ the ship doth keep —
Oh blessed Saints! ye woke your Lord
  From that mysterious sleep.

Oh blessed Saints! I am fast bound
  By sins of youthful days —
Ye could unbind the graveclothes once
  Of him your Lord did raise.

I know there is one Mother yet
  (Changed Mother! dost *thou* not know?)
Who never bade a sorrowing child
  In hopeless sorrow go.

I know that I am not alone
  Her prayers ascend each hour —
I think, oh thou my soul doth love!
  She hath Thy Heavenly dower.

Oh Blessed Lord! may I and mine
Be with the One True Mother:
Then what Thou wilt-to gift of Thee
  I cannot ask another!

Trin. Coll. Oct. 21st, 1845.

II. IRELAND AND THE OXFORD MOVEMENT

The Oxford Movement had connection with Ireland, but the academical travail of an English University was necessarily remote from Ireland's own revivals during the Victorian century. The Oxford Movement was essentially a part of English history but even so Ireland has her way of intruding across the Channel. In the first place it is noteworthy that the Tractarians were inspired by the Anglo-Irish Bishops Jebb and Mant, and by Alexander Knox, who had been a convert of Wesley and had preserved the high ideals of the Nonjurors. Charles Leslie their Pamphleteer had been an Irish Cleric. The Anglo-Irish Church was not yet Evangelical or under the Orange influence. It was the privileged and careless Church of the ruling class. Her Bishops were Whigs, Englishmen or scoundrels mingled with a few fine old Irish gentlemen. Their enemies were Presbyterian and they inclined to protect the poor Catholic on whom they lived. The Catholic Bishops were imbued with continental culture and some of them were Government men. Dr. Doyle, their ablest spokesman, proposed Reunion and, strange as it may appear, Bishop Jebb, a Protestant, was allowed to address a Roman congregation on the same subject after Mass. But this was in the spacious days of O'Connell and before Cardinal Cullen had swept Ireland with an Ultramontane broom.

The Oxford men failed to influence the Anglo-Irish clergy who became alarmed or sarcastic. But there were signs and examples. St. Columba's was started to keep the sons of landlords in Ireland in an atmosphere of High Church and Celtic learning. The pupils wore surplices and chanted grace in Irish. Irish High Churchmen claimed to represent the Celtic Church before Rome disciplined Ireland. For the second time in history the Anglo-Irish laid claim to St. Patrick. Two Irish Churchmen visiting Rome apologised to Pius for being Protestants. "No matter," laughed the Pope, "I will mention it to St. Patrick."

Irish studies arose largely in the patronage of enlightened men like Bishop Reeves, who saved the Book of Armagh; or Dr. Todd of Trinity, who wrote a Biography claiming St. Patrick for the Church of Ireland; or Evelyn Shirley, the liturgical collector whom Disraeli described as "Mr. Ardenne"; or Lord Dunraven, who sumptuously described Irish Architecture; or Aubrey de Vere, who turned Gaelic legends into Tennysonian verse. Dunraven and De Vere became Catholics. From Trinity, Dublin, came William Palmer, who gave the Tractarians his knowledge of the Primitive Liturgies.

Irish High Churchmen sought livings on the other side of the Channel. The type of Jebb, who inspired the Sacramentalism in the Tracts, and Knox, who according to Newman foresaw the great restoration, died out. Isolated Tractarians took their place like Canon MacIlwaine of St. George's, Belfast, Dr. Maturin of Grangegorman, and Canon Young of Ballybay, who held their own in the face of fierce Orange protests. Greatest of Irish Tractarians was Dr. Alexander, who had followed Newman almost unto Birmingham, but who became Bishop of Derry and finally Primate in the Anglo-Irish Church. Against his courageous and loving protest the Sign of the Cross was swept from the Holy Table after Disestablishment in 1870 and the Prayer Book revised so as to expunge the least excuse for Ritualists. The Orange Churchmen were led by Lord James Butler, who "wished to belong to an Episcopal Church without Bishops."

The High Churchmen refused to sign the panicky Canons, which have a comic touch when read to-day. A Mohammedan Committee might have drawn up the Canon against the Cross. Another was directed against the use of Incense or "any substitute for Incense," whatever that might be! The Cross was forbidden to be placed on or behind the altar. Dr. Maturin ingeniously placed it in front! When Lord Carson forced the Vicar of St. Bartholomew's, Dublin, to remove the Cross from his altar, he suspended it from wire so that it hung an inch above! St. Bartholomew's and St. John's Sandymount held out with an advanced Ritual defying Bishop or mob. For the young High Churchmen Ireland seemed to offer little choice save Rome or exile.

The famous Dr. Littledale came from Trinity, Dublin. He was an encyclopædia of controversy, sketched in a novel as "Dr. O'Frothie." His *Plain Reasons* against Rome were best answered by Father Ryder. He said Mass daily and patronised a Community of Sisters. Next to Pusey he was the most consulted of Anglican confessors.

The Revisers had removed all lessons taken from the Apocrypha and kenelled the Athanasian Creed. They knocked out the Absolution from the Visitation of the Sick as "a form unknown to the Church in ancient times." It was told that an Irish Protestant Vestry would only accept a stained-glass window of Solomon on condition that he was bearded, lest he might be mistaken for the Virgin Mary! Canon Young described the excitements on his life in his *Memoirs:* how he only kept a Cross over his wife's grave by threatening the rate-payers with the cost of every successive desecration. Archbishop Plunket of Dublin and Bishop Stack of Clogher attempted to drive a coach-and-six through the Branch theory by setting out to Spain and ordaining a Reformed Hiberno-Anglican Bishop for the Peninsula! This brought a grave apology from Lord Halifax and the English Church Union to the surprised Spanish Cardinals, who really did not mind whether the Irish Protestant Bishops stood on their heads in the bullring or not.

The Prayer Book of the Irish Church is not likely ever to be revised in a High Church sense and may be regarded as a permanent defeat of the Oxford School. Its history deserves to be written. It was the Book accepted by the Irish Bishops after the Savoy Conference of 1662 with the addition (now abandoned) of a melancholy service for October 23, the outbreak of the Irish Rebellion of 1641. The Protestantism of the Church of Ireland became thereafter stereotyped. The Caroline Irish Bishops had been High Church with a strong bias against Presbyterians. The title of "Church of Ireland" was gradually substituted for Church of England, which was its original appellative. Previously the Irish Prayer Book was the English one printed in Ireland. Protestants find it difficult to believe that the First Prayer Book of King Edward was introduced into Ireland in 1551 with the word *Mass*. It proved such a foreign book that under Elizabeth Common Prayer was permitted in Latin owing to lack of English-speaking Ministers. The claim to be the Primitive Church of Ireland was a legacy of the Caroline Bishops, and to be the Church of St. Patrick an after-thought, supported by scholars from Ussher to Todd, but not likely to be accepted by the Protestant laity until St. Patrick's colour can be shewn a truer Blue than suspected! Professor Bury, son of an Irish Rectory, inclined to surrender the National Saint to the opinion of Roman Divines in his masterly *St. Patrick*.

On the whole the Oxford Movement left Ireland cold. The only Tracts which reached the people were Protestant. The Irish parsons, who left for Rome, could be counted on five fingers. The first Irish Tractarian, William Henn, left after a stormy career. His chest was afterwards found "full of false gods!" It was claimed that a carriage umbrella could always cover the assembled Ritualists of Dublin. Convert priests were regarded by the natives with amused suspicion. When one spoke of Purgatory as the effulgence from Mary's throne, the congregation burst into laughter. They had heard it described otherwise!

On the other hand, in Wales and Scotland, where the background was Calvinist, the isolated Anglican Churches were deeply tinctured by the Oxford Movement. The

Scotch branch had remained Nonjuror until 1788 and to-day represents a self-contained High Church in full blossom. From Scotland came a series of English Primates: Tait, Davidson, and Lang, all of the blood of the Manse. The only Irish Archbishop was Magee, in the See of York. During the controversy over Anglican Orders the piquant fact came to the surface that the Anglo-Irish Bishops were not descended from Barlow at all but from Curwen, Queen Mary's Archbishop of Dublin, whose consecration derived (tell it not in Portadown nor whisper it in Belfast!) from the Romanists Bonner and Gardiner!

III. RELIGIOUS ORDERS IN THE CHURCH OF ENGLAND

The Oxford Movement brought the Religious Orders back to England. For a century they have steadily grown under both Roman and Anglican flags. They are more numerous to-day than under Henry VIII, after suffering complete obliteration. The first Cistercians to return wore wigs over their shaven heads to soothe Protestant feelings. The Benedictines, with a succession from Westminster itself, for the Heralds granted them the old arms, built Abbeys at Downside in Somerset and Ampleforth in Yorkshire. Other Benedictine Abbeys were restored at Quarr and Buckfast. The Carthusians brought the *Grande Chartreuse* into Sussex. The Friars, Franciscan and Dominican, poured into Parish work. The Jesuits set camp at Oxford and Berkeley Square. Over a hundred converts became Jesuits. At Beaumont and Stonyhurst they tempered the English Public School with the *Exercises* of Ignatius Loyola. The Benedictines entered into the lists of the Public School at Downside, Ampleforth, and Douai. Newman's Oratory School now faces the ruins of Reading Abbey. The Convents of women are innumerable where a century ago they were scarcely known or rumoured to exist.

Nor have the Anglicans been idle. Miss Sellon was the first Anglican nun. Canon Carter at Clewer, Butler at Wantage, and Dr. Neale at East Grinstead founded famous Communities of Sisters. The Cholera and the Crimean War reversed the unpopularity of nuns and religious dress. Both Churches can claim a record of heroism. Near Oxford Father R. M. Benson founded the Cowley Fathers, who have tried to combine the wisdom of Jesuits with the innocence of Franciscans. In the 'Nineties Father Kelly founded the Sacred Mission for bringing poor students to priesthood. Dr. Gore founded the Community of the Resurrection and Father Adderly founded that of the Divine Compassion. Dr. Gore became Bishop of Birmingham and one of his successors at Mirfield, Bishop of Truro: both appointed by the State. Mirfield mingles the Benedictine and Redemptorist.

In the list of Anglican Communities there is one real tragedy catalogued under the simple words:

"Order of St. Benedict. Rev. J. L. Lyne, 1863."

Mr. Lyne, as Father Ignatius, aspired to restore the religious life for men, as Mother Sellon had done for women. Both suffered from the mob and ignorant Bishops. In an Episcopal enquiry Miss Sellon was accused of calling Pusey "father" and Friday a festival day! Bishops tormented poor Lyne and refused him Ordination to priesthood. He declined to abandon his mingled dress of Monk and Friar at Wilberforce's command. Like General Booth he wanted a striking uniform and new methods. He preached the same Salvationism, but varied his mission, it was said, by raising a girl from the dead with a Relic of the True Cross. This was thought uncalled for in an Anglican Curate. For fifty years he bore the brunt of familiarising the public with the religious habit which

Catholics kept to privacy. He bore the violence and hatred of the day, like the lightning conductor of the Oxford Movement. He appeared in Rome with an elderly nun and an adopted child clad in sandals and white habit. A Benedictine baby flustered Rome, and Pope Pius sent to Ignatius to tell him kindly that a cowl did not make a monk. Ignatius became a fashionable preacher, while his monks starved at Llanthony, though consoled for their Superior's absence by occasional apparitions. Our Lady was described appearing to children, as at Lourdes to Bernadette. Eventually there arrived one Mar Timotheus, a roving Jacobite Bishop, who had supervised the Old Catholic sect in America. His was hardly a proper standing from which to ordain an English monk in a Welsh Diocese, but Father Ignatius received valid Orders, for Rome recognises, though against the grain, the Orders of Jacobite, Syriac and Old Catholic. The Monks of Llanthony came and went. Finally they all went and the body of their founder lies buried in his deserted Church. Some of the monks joined the Caldey Benedictines founded by Dom Carlyle in 1895, but as no Anglican Bishop would take responsibility these passed to Roman pastures. Besides the alleged vision at Llanthony no other was recorded in an Anglican Community save by Dr. Neale, who believed he was once rebuked by Our Lord in the Quadrangle of Sackville College.

The Cowley Fathers have been the most successful Anglican Order of men. They have spread to Boston, Bombay, and Capetown. Members of the Society have become Bishops of Vermont and Fond du Lac. Their founder was a mystic and a bureaucrat. One member, Father Long-ridge, wrote a remarkable commentary on the Exercises of St. Ignatius. Basil Maturin and Luke Rivington of the Fathers have come over to Rome. Mirfield boasts that its only loss was Mgr. Benson.

Anglican Sisterhoods have far outnumbered the Houses for men. They were signalled as far back as 1841, when Newman celebrated in St. Mary's at the dedication of a Miss Hughes. Pusey's daughter wished to be a nun and her death led Pusey to father Sisterhoods. Naturally they were a puzzle and a distress to Victorian Bishops. Wilber-force turned the tide in their favour while insisting they should not take vows. They have since become as great an estate in the Church of England as the Bishops them-selves.

Neale was the most typical of Anglican founders, for he combined it with domestic life and added his daughters by the flesh to his daughters in Christ. He endured inhibi-tion by his Bishop and the attentions of the mob, who rioted twice at Sisters' funerals. Though the Crimean War damped his proposed reunion with the Greek Church, the Cholera gave his Sisters the chance to make good the love of the people, whom his Bishop accused him of debasing with "spiritual haberdashery." He held a quaint theory of the Triple Rock of Peter: "Antioch where he sat, Alex-andria which he superintended, Rome where he suf-ferred." His panegyric of the Byzantine and Greek once drew a cheque from the Czar. Neale could not help com-paring the East with "the happy flexibility of the Church of Rome. That Church begins with hermits: she forms them into communities and they become monks. She sends them into the world and they are Friars. She bids them to go to great men and speak and they are Jesuits. In an ignorant age the Benedictine went into his garden and planted cabbages. In a learned age he sat in his cell and edited the Fathers." So wrote Neale in 1850. Within half a century there were monks at Parkminster and Grace-dieu, Friars in English parishes and suburbs, Jesuits mocking Fashion in Mayfair or wrestling with Learning at Oxford, English Benedictines editing the Vulgate. But these were all under Papal jurisdiction. Communities for men have never been a great success in the Church of England. For the expenditure of men and money the results have been small. But the Orders of women have kept pace with their Roman sisters. Neale saw the Church of England rising like Lazarus and, though the Anglican revival of monkery smelt of the grave, Martha and Mary returned to work or contemplation as of old.

IV. THE OXFORD MOVEMENT IN ARCHITECTURE

The Oxford Movement marked town and countryside when transferred to architecture. Horace Walpole and Walter Scott had bred a false and artificial dawn to the Gothic Revival which burst into sudden noon with Pugin. The eccentric Beckford built as wildly as a mediæval master builder in the void, but what he called "the march of the true faith" had not come in his time. Pugin, converted by his mad love of Gothic, restored and built at fever pace. He was a superb decorator and revived colour in churches. His was the rediscovery of polychromatic work. With a coat of many colours he bespread English churches. His was the entire decoration of the Houses of Parliament, though the descendants of Barry, for whom he worked, concealed the debt. His were the Cathedrals of St. George in Southwark and St. Chad in Birmingham. His were forty splendid churches through the land. He had time to marry thrice and died at forty leaving his fiery Gothic spirit to inspire or challenge every Church-builder in Britain.

He wrought with pen as well as with pencil. His invective was such that he was constrained to be his own publisher. He cried aloud with horror at the restored English Cathedrals. Take for example Salisbury where he noted:

"the destruction of the Hungerford and Beauchamp Chapels: the demolition of the Screen which separated the Lady Chapel from the Choir: the destruction of the Saints' Chapels in the West transept and of the Roodloft before the Choir: the removal of the monuments in order to line the arcades of the Nave." The reader can now understand why Salisbury looks like a stone barn with the tombs distributed like Museum exhibits. Hereford he found restored by the appalling Cockney architect Wyatt: "What do you think of a regular Roman altar screen, a modern window over it with the Last Supper from West like a great transparency!" Wyatt as late as 1780 had scattered the stained glass of Salisbury until it found a resting place in the town ditch.

Pugin's *Contrasts* was one of the most laughable and delicious books ever printed. He drew accusing sketches of mediæval and modern architecture side by side: of the best Gothic and the worst Georgian. He set the High Altar of Hereford, looking like a Railway Buffet in 1830, beside Durham as it was in 1430. He compared Nash's ridiculous Temple at the top of Regent Street with St. Mary's Redcliffe, and the Chapel Royal at Brighton in action with St. George's Windsor in Catholic days. He drew the lovely tomb of Admiral Alard at Winchelsea beside the recumbent figure on a modern monument swathed in dressing gown, looking like a victim of bathroom apoplexy. Finally he compared the Catholic Bishop of Ely's Palace in Holborn with the Protestant Bishop's house with its nursery windows: and "all useless buildings such as Chapel omitted." It was amusingly unfair and caused furious resentment, for like a true Goth Pugin attacked St. Paul's in London as well as St. Peter's in Rome. He carried the Gothic Cult to delicious lengths, refusing to believe the Virgin could appear to Fr. Ratisbonne in a Church that was not Gothic and dissuading a Priest from the uselessness of praying for the conversion of England in a modern cope!

But as Purcell said, "Pugin was the Gibbon of Architecture. In the *Contrasts* he wrote the history of the Decline and Fall." He neatly said that one half of St. Paul's was built to conceal the other half. He promoted softly flowing Gothic vestments against the stiff Italian tabards which Roman and Anglican love. He called the London Oratory "the shilling opera house" in his fierce crusade for Plain Chant and mediæval music. This Crusade was one day justified by Pius X. Although he described the Sistine as "a melancholy room, the Last Judgment painfully muscular, the *Scala Regia* humbug," and thought St. Peter's not a Christian Church at all, the Pope gave him a gold medal. Pugin was rejected by the Royal Academy, because he was a genius, and by Balliol because he was a Catholic, with the result that Balliol was rebuilt by men of irreproachable sentiments, but without genius; a type she has never ceased to produce. He prepared the magnificent mediæval section of the Great Exhibition in 1851, which gave John Bull his first taste for Ritualism. Soon afterwards his brimming brain broke and he was laid under one of his own beautiful buildings. His sermons were in stone and as the *Times* admitted: "Pugin is dead. It was he who first showed us that our Architecture offended not only against the law of beauty but also against the laws of morality."

On two occasions the Oxford Movement met genius: in John Henry Newman and in Augustus Welby Pugin. Both were exquisite converts and masters of style. Both found themselves stumbling against the prevailing Italianism, whether in devotion or architecture. Newman was as much troubled by Ultramontanes as Pugin was by the ultra-pagan builders who have possessed the Church since the Renaissance. Pugin was suppressed in life by Barry and obliterated in death by Ruskin, who was determined to give Gothic a Protestant lease. But Pugin worked for his cause careless to whom went the honour. The same unresting hand which gave England the first Cistercian monastery erected since the Reformation left Oscott with "the finest Paschal candlestick in Europe" and Westminster with the soaring stonework called Big Ben. During the decade preceding the return of the Hierarchy Pugin passed through England insanely inspired, making the House of God more beautiful and ornate than the English thought proper, and crying aloud: "make Gothic the paths of the Lord and with pointed Architecture prepare the road of His Coming!"

Mr. Goodhart Rendell, in his *Vitruvian Nights,* dates 1859 as the change from Pugin and imitation of Gothic to Ruskin and a mixed choice in styles. "Pugin, the Movement's chief apostle, had submitted to the Church of Rome and was therefore not regarded as an eligible consultant by most of the Clergy of the Establishment. Carpenter, Butterfield, Harrison, and Pearson were trusted architects, who could be counted to go no further than Puseyism, while for those that demanded Protestant security Sir Gilbert Scott, Ferrey, and Salvin were reliable guides." This slightly satirical summary records the history of the Oxford Movement in architecture. But Scott was simply a worshipper of the Puginesque. The English were always stupendous Church builders. Remark the twenty-four grandiose Cathedrals in a smaller area than any abroad. Remark the mediæval rivalry between parish and parish in East Anglia, only to be compared to the modern zeal between Roman and Anglican Structures, which is finding its climax in the two gigantic Cathedrals of Liverpool: the Anglican built by a Catholic and the Catholic designed as yet by a non-Catholic. Since the Reformation the Church of England has added three Cathedrals: Liverpool, St. Paul's, and Truro built by Pearson. In the track of Pugin came the famous firm of Bodley and Garner, to be dissolved when Garner followed Pugin's religious example as well. Gilbert Scott's stonework became as definitely Anglican as Kempe's stained windows so that all over the world, wherever Anglican Chaplaincies or Bishoprics were installed, the architectural print of the Oxford Movement arose in the land. Scott was a Philistine compared to Street, who restored York and Carlisle Cathedrals. Both Keble and Pusey were commemorated amongst Oxford buildings. Newman and Manning have their memorial elsewhere. Most of Scott's multitudinous work was performed by "Ghosts." But Pugin pencilled every inch to the last crocket and the least tendril. Pugin fought for a national Gothic style but under Ruskin's influence the Romanesque and the Basilican entered England. Screens and Chancels gave way to flat roofs and cornices. Newman had John Pollen build a Basilica in Dublin, the opposite pole to Pugin's Gothic gem at Enniscorthy. The climax came when Bentley built a magnificent *Sancta Sophia* with a Campanile at Westminster to outbulk and outrage both St. Edward's Abbey and Pugin's Cathedral in Southwark. The Oratory at Brompton was at least a Latin Church, one in which Beardsley said he could forget the existence of the London Sunday!

The race of great church-builders came to an end with Sir Tatton Sykes, who littered Yorkshire with Anglican Gothic and even promised Cardinal Manning to reproduce the Votive Church at Vienna as a Cathedral in Westminster. With difficulty he was persuaded that even the Sledmere Stud could not stand the quarter of a million necessary. But it was owing to this prospect that the site of the present Cathedral was purchased. After Lord Shrewsbury came Henry Duke of Norfolk, who will be remembered as a Church-builder long after his politics are forgotten. He added the great Cathedral-like structures at Arundel and Norwich, living a devout and defiant mediæval figure in Court or Parliament. His *Life* by Bernard Holland has unfortunately not been allowed to appear. As a hereditary Catholic he met the Oxford Movement with true nobility and by his steadfast influence obtained Cardinal Newman his Hat.

V. THE OXFORD MOVEMENT IN LITERATURE

The effect of the Oxford Movement upon literature was immense, taking the works of Newman alone. At one moment Oxford lay between Newman and Arnold, "his great opposite," who had been brought into a Chair of History to disperse Tractarianism forever. On the threshold of his attack he died leaving his Life and his Liberalism to Stanley, who himself was conquered by Newman's style. His sons, Matthew and Thomas Arnold, were conquered no less, and Thomas even followed Newman to Dublin and after three changes died a Catholic.

As Newman had offered Oxford Religion, Jowett offered her Plato, Matthew Arnold, Poetry, and finally Ruskin, Art. These were pretty substitutes for Newmanism. They were all impregnated with his ideas. Every subsequent Movement was begotten in Newman's wake. Oxford youth was stamped with the image of Newman if not on the obverse on the reverse of the medal. Even after his departure he powerfully affected Oxford while in the throes of Reform by writing his *Idea of a University*. Written in the dull atmosphere of Dublin it fell like a glittering mantle upon the pinnacles of the City which he loved more even than Rome. Whately's *Cautions for the Times,* which he and Salmon were inditing from Dublin at this time, never left the Liffey. Newman's standard still floated over the Isis. Reform was the penalty which the Protestant State exacted from the Puseyite University. Anglican sinecures and privileges were abolished. The Universities were nationalised and the Church of England driven back upon her intellectual lines, where Dissenter and Liberal for different reasons were less able to grapple with her.

But for lack of Newman's pen the Church Party were unable to hold their Oxford Citadel. As soon as the Tractarian Movement ceased to kindle the University, others took its place. Matthew Arnold literally brought English Poetry to a University whose official language had been a crabbed Latin. He laid down Criticism by which literature could be estimated without thought of religion. The tide-gates were now open. Newman begat Matthew Arnold, and Arnold begat Ruskin, and Ruskin begat the Pre-Raphaelites, Morris and Rossetti and Burne-Jones, who were all the children or adopted of Oxford. And Morris begat Pater, and Pater begat Wilde, so that even the Æsthetic Movement can be traced to the first stirrings of unearthly beauty awakened by the Vicar of St. Mary's.

The Oxford Movement was not slow to slip into the novels. A time came when novels took the place of Tracts in England. It is curious that Dickens never described the Parson, except as part of the Christmas decorations. Oxford was nothing to him as a child of the people and his satire was reserved for the Dissenting Chadbands and Jellabies. Thackeray described how Newman gave up his fame and leadership. The Church interiors in the plates of *David Copperfield* exactly show what Church furniture was before the Movement. Newman himself spun the Oxford warfare into *Loss and Gain,* which, read between the lines, is a closer *Apologia* than the flaming spear which he loosed at Kingsley twenty years later. Newman's *Callista,* like Wiseman's *Fabiola,* was an attempt to teach early Christian history to English readers. The most profoundly affected of Novelists by the Oxford Movement was Disraeli. The splendour of Victorian days was such that Cardinals and Prime Ministers wrote novels. In the year of Newman's going out Disraeli issued *Sybil,* rich in the picture of the Chartists and of aristocratic life in a dismantled Abbey. His scorn for the Church of the Squirarchy appears: "Oligarchy has been called Liberty, an exclusive Priesthood has been christened a National Church." Never were the ruins or memories of a great English Abbey more nobly described than Marney Abbey: "The eyes of this unhappy race might have been raised to the solitary spire that sprang up in the midst of them, the bearer of present consolation, the harbinger of future equality, but Holy Church at Marney had forgotten her sacred mission." Was Disraeli also amongst the Tractarians? He compared the old mitred Abbeys to "thirty or forty Chatsworths, the proprietors of which were never absent. The monks were never non-resident. They made the country beautiful and the people proud of their country. The monasteries were taken by storm. Never was such a plunder. It was worse than the Norman Conquest nor has England ever lost this character of ravage. I don't know whether the Union Workhouses will remove it."

The Labour Movement as well as the Catholic Revival dates with the printing of *Sybil*. But Disraeli was appealing to the Young Englanders, to the scions of nobility to redeem their people and their Church by inspiring serf and curate. His own career as a future Bishop-maker was veiled or he might not have let the fascination of Rome shine in his pages.

It is worth making a little summary of this sidetrack in his Oriental mind. May Dacre in the *Young Duke* is a Catholic heroine like *Sybil*. He wins her by championing Catholic Emancipation. *Contarini Fleming,* the shadow of Disraeli himself, and Eustace de Lyle (Ambrose de Lisle) are all Roman converts. In de Lyle, the mentor of *Coningsby,* the Oxford and Young England Movements met both in book and reality. *Tancred* exposes the deficiencies of the English Church and *Sybil* is haunted by what the Roman might do to emancipate the English people. In *Tancred* he scorns the Protestantising of Ireland as well as Bishop Blomfield of London. In *Lothair* he describes imaginary intrigues for the conversion of Lord Bute, with Manning as Cardinal Grandison, in great irony. Manning and Bishop Wilberforce, with "seraphic raillery and angelic jokes," contend for Lothair's soul, while Monsignor Capel (who received Lord Bute) was disguised as Mgr. Catesby. The Nigel Penruddock of *Endymion* was a revised sketch of Manning: "the prophet who had been ordained in Mayfair" and might have been a Dean had he not gone over to Rome and become the Archbishop of Tyre. Disraeli thought Transubstantiation too good to be true. His early thought was probably his last on the subject: "All other Churches established by the Hebrew Apostles have disappeared but Rome remains."

An Anglican Prelate once described the religious novel as an unfortunate mixture of two good things, which he preferred to take apart like sherry and port. The religious novel became as predominant at one time as its successor the sex-story. Miss Austen's famous gallery of Curates was Pre-Tractarian. All except "Mr. Collins" were gentlemen. They hunted for partners rather than souls. Charlotte Yonge poured best-sellers forth from the sanctuary of Keble's parish. From the Catholic side came Lady Georgiana Fullerton's *Ellen Middleton*. Trollope used High and Low for his clerical Gallery. In the *Warden* he alludes to Sir Abraham Hayward's Bill for the mortification of Papists and describes the Hon. and Rev. Vesey Stanhope, who combined Stall and Rectory with a villa on Lake Como and possessed a unique collection of butterflies. Kingsley's *Yeast* has a Tractarian Curate who is casuist enough to alter fact to suit the common vision. Kingsley in *Westward Ho* and Reade in the *Cloister and the Hearth* made Priests the villains, thwarting the old instincts and persecuting the new knowledge, although Reade's was in other ways a powerful mediæval novel. Kingsley caricatured the Elizabethan Jesuits, Parsons and Campion, with sincere malevolence. Mrs. Humphrey Ward's *Robert Elsmere* was a fair picture of the Broad Church reaction, which Gladstone reviewed as though he were reading a Gospel according to the doubting Thomas. The moral of the book was that miracles do not happen,

which is no doubt true. If miracles merely happened they
would not be miracles. The High Churchman is described
by Mrs. Ward as one who would "die for an alb," while
the well-meaning parson loses his faith through a little
indiscreet reading in his Squire's library. The best-drawn
High Churchman is to be found in Hall Caine's *Christian*.
A later sensation, *When it was Dark*, by Guy Thorne has
pictures of Lord Halifax and Mr. Kensit as rival protago-
nists of Anglican Churchmanship. On the Roman side
were two admirable novelists: Mrs. Wilfrid Ward, whose
Out of Due Time was the antidote to the other Mrs.
Ward, the daughter of Arnold, and Mrs. Craigie, who
wrote with fashionable orthodoxy as "John Oliver
Hobbes." The finest religious novel of the century was
John Inglesant, written by a Birmingham Quaker, in
which the hero wavers between Caroline divines and mel-
odramatic Jesuits. It presented a colourful tapestry of the
Seventeenth Century, out of the threads of which Lord
Acton drew scores of anachronisms, but it gave High
Churchmen both dream and inspiration. It presented a
misty quintessence of the Oxford Movement in historical
guise. The executions of Laud and King Charles, the
apparition of Strafford, the Papal Conclave, the Anglican
nuns at Little Gidding, the famous scenes in which the
hero resists taking advantage of the heroine or slaying his
brother's murderer, made it an Anglican masterpiece. Almost it might explain the Anglican soul to the Latin
mind. It was an attempt to show how little apparently lay
between the Churches, for John Inglesant can be the mystical subject of one and the political tool of the other. But

what strange Jesuits! such as never yet on land or sea! Better almost condemn the Society with Pascal than absolve them with John Inglesant. The religious influence of the book was immense and abiding. Birmingham was rich in prophets in the 'Eighties.

Newman's *Loss and Gain* must be reckoned the Novel of the Movement *par excellence.* Therein he pictured people and events that he knew from experience. The great leader describes himself in Charles Reding and tells the agony of his last parting from Oxford:

"There was no one to see him: he threw his arms round the willows so dear to him and kissed them; he tore off some of their black leaves and put them in his bosom."

Other passages are famous: the description of the light conversation and heavy fasting fare at the Oxford Tutor's breakfast, and the suggestion of marriage compared to the offer of a pork chop during sea-sickness on the Channel! A Key has been supplied by W. H. Mallock to his *New Republic,* which describes a brilliant symposium of the post-Newman Oxford. It covers the aftermath of the Movement and some celebrated Left-overs speak for themselves, such as Jowett (Dr. Jenkinson) who absurdly says, "true Christianity embraces all opinion even any honest denial of itself": Huxley (Mr. Storks) the spearpoint of the Darwinian thesis: Ruskin (Mr. Herbert) the scarecrow of the Philistines: Matthew Arnold (Mr. Luke) who never shed the influence of Newman, but who preferred to war against Philistines rather than Protestants: Pater (Mr.

Rose) the father of the Æsthetes and trainer of many a literary Adonis. The Church of Rome was represented by the "daughter of old Sir Ascot Merton the horse-racing Evangelical."

In Mgr. Hugh Benson the English Catholics found their novelist historical, contemporary and apocalyptic, for he dipped his pen through all periods. He was inspired by *John Inglesant* and by the astonishing Baron Corvo, whose autobiographical novel *Hadrian VII,* which might be rendered "If I were Pope," had swept him off his feet. Corvo, whose Anglican name had been Rolfe, was a convert of the most æsthetic school. A key to *Hadrian VII* reveals contemporary English Catholics and the Papal Conclave of 1903 seen through an opera glass darkly. It remains the most ecclesiastical novel ever written but strangely compacted by genius and vulgarity. Corvo's influence led Benson into the paths of the morbid and the magnificent. His psychological studies of moody young men were taken from life, but his females of wax and ink were taken from the manikins in shop-windows. For him the feminine was merely an obstacle or a ladder spiritually. His only heroine was Queen Mary, whom he treated as originally and fearlessly as Shaw later dealt with Joan of Arc. The other Monsignor Novelist was Bickerstaffe Drew, who deserved a novel to mirror his own peculiarities. He was described as a Catholic Trollope, which carries both his over-praise and his criticism. His best book was *San Celestino,* a Papal lyric in novel form. The clash between Roman and Anglican was maliciously drawn by Richard Bagot in *The Casting of Nets,* in which the convert Lady Herbert of Lea was parodied. It was like Disraeli's *Lothair* without Disraeli's grace.

The Æsthetic Movement sometimes resembles a pagan offshoot of the Oxford Movement. At its commencement the influences on art and poetry were all religious. Ruskin graduated during the Tracts and returned after the flight of the Tractarians as Professor of Fine Arts. Ruskin has proved one of the most notable of Victorian collapses, but once he bulked to swollen proportions. He found a Bible in Amiens and made a Psalter of the Stones of Venice. His Guild of St. George was a brave, single-handed effort to mediævalise and beautify the increasing squalor of English life. He tried, as all the Oxford men tried, to bring his teaching to the service of the people. He inspired William Morris and Burne-Jones, and their coloured glass and tapestry must be gathered to any museum of the Movement. Ruskin remained a mediæval Guildsman, but Morris became a pioneer of Socialism. Ruskin was patron to the Pre-Raphaelites and the later æsthetes were fledged from under his winged umbrella. As for the Catholic Church, he was too fascinated by her golden embroidery and sandals to look her in the face. He was delightfully inconsequent and bewildered himself into madness. He caused equally the triumph and the failure of Gothic. When he taught Oscar Wilde the art of road-making, he was passing the wand of beauty to a school who had little thought of plying it amongst the poor and humble. The Tractarian and Æsthetic Movements met when Canon

MacIlwaine published Wilde's poems for the first time in book form in an Anthology of sacred Irish song, in 1878.

Pre-Raphaelite poets included Coventry Patmore, who attained heights and depths, which Tennyson generally avoided, and Christina Rossetti, a Dantesque figure reduced to the stature of an Anglican pew-opener.

The great Poets were not blind to the Oxford Movement. And Dean Hutton wrote: "No one can think that Tennyson was wholly unmoved by its manner: but Dolben and Pater were the undoubted issue of its later life." Browning's satire on Bishop Blougram was meant for Wiseman.

The greatest of the Oxford æsthetes was Walter Pater who remained an Anglican like Christina, but of his pious paganism there could be no doubt. He was a master of words and of Wilde. He lipsticked the lily and painted charming miniatures upon white marble. *Marius the Epicurean,* his masterpiece, was an Oxford dilletante who died on the road between Marcus Aurelius and Christ. Pater himself died on the road between Pusey and Leo XIII, because he lingered too long in the way at the Sign of the Giaconda. Other æsthetes lingered in the Street of the Seven Deadly Sins. Living his protected life in the shadow of the University, without academic responsibility, Pater never saw sufficient of the world's evil to substitute Satan for Pan. Unexorcised by the Tractarians, and invisible to the Proctors, Pan lurked in the thickets of the Isis and even trod College lawns unseen at night. Pater was content to sell his beautiful wares outside the Gate of

Beauty, through which his disciple Wilde was to trudge in convict's dress. The imprisonment in Reading Gaol gave England the most beautiful and penitential Sequence written since the Middle Ages. Wilde sought Catholic symbols to cover his disgrace, even finding a memory of St. Sebastian in the Broad Arrows upon his prison clothes. For two decades the Æsthetic Movement filled English Literature and occasional stalls in the Catholic Church. The finer flower yielded converts like Lionel Johnson and Gerard Hopkins. Hopkins became a Jesuit and invented an exquisite technique in which modern verse has found its prelude and prophesy.

The Oxford Movement gave a stimulus to historical study, for every school of thought was anxious to find its title-deeds. The University produced Froude, Freeman and Stubbs. Froude tried to canonise Henry VIII. Stubbs overthrew this hero-worship, while Freeman spent his life overthrowing Froude. Brewer complained that scarcely a statement in Froude's story of the early life of Thomas Cromwell was correct. When Froude turned to attack the Irish Catholics, Lecky entirely dismantled him. Such was the career of a disgruntled Newmanite! Stubbs, who became a Bishop, and Freeman were High Churchmen. Maitland, who was neither Anglican nor Roman, proved against Stubbs that England had been really subject to Roman Canon Law. Anglicans had hoped in a tradition of independence from the Holy See.

The Catholic historians were all Catholic-born: Lingard, Acton, Gasquet. Lingard wrote outside the Movement and some thought almost outside the Church, so lukewarm were his feelings to Becket and Joan of Arc. Though he did not appear always to champion Right he was never proved in the wrong. Acton was a real stumblingblock to Catholics, though he traced all the happiness and greatness that modern men have achieved to the Middle Ages. His fierce love of Liberty led him to attack Protestantism on the very two points usually hurled against the Catholic Church: the freedom of conscience and the practice of persecution. The authorities never realised how profound and subtle a champion they possessed and preferred to aggravate him into opposition. The two greatest sons of the Oxford Movement, Newman and Gladstone, sent their pitchers to his well-head. The years brought an unexpected finale to his life. He died in the Cambridge Chair of History unexcommunicated!

Hymns can only be accounted literature for the purposes of religion. The Oxford Movement was prolific in Hymns, Hymnals, and Hymnology. Of the world-famous collection *Hymns Ancient and Modern* a half are due to the Movement and the new sources of inspiration. Previously the Church of England relied on metrical versions of the Psalms of David, of which it could only be said that Uriah could not invoke a bitterer revenge. Asked what a Drysalter was Sam Wilberforce wittily remarked Tate and Brady! Neale was the greatest of Hymn-writers in the Anglican ranks. Two Hymn-writers, Bridges and Caswall, left for Rome. But Hymns were long thought dangerous, for Bishop Marsh of Peterborough spent £ 4,000 preventing a clergyman introducing a hymn-book in the days when even eagle lecterns and Harvest Thanksgivings were accounted Popish!

The Oxford Movement produced a Press apart from the famous Periodicals associated with Newman and Acton and Wiseman (*Rambler, Home and Foreign Review,* and *Dublin*). Lord Blachford, a friend of Newman, founded the *Guardian* which, with the *Saturday Review,* upheld the dignity of the Anglican Faith. The *Church Times* became the flaming oriflamme of the Anglo-Catholics while the *Record* hammered on the other side. The *Tablet* was Rome's vigilant champion. Founded by a convert, Frederick Lucas, it enjoyed an Irish youth but under Herbert Vaughan adopted a severely English outlook. The Irish Catholics in England have their own organs while the *Universe* preserves a sagacious balance. So much for a Press which would scarcely be in circulation had not the Tractarians once written their Tracts. No periodical thrived more on the Movement, than *Punch* from which Dicky Doyle resigned as a protest in Wiseman's day. A volume only could contain the caricatures and attacks on Roman and Anglican until a later editor, Burnand, included amongst his "Happy Thoughts" that of becoming Catholic.

The Oxford Movement has not been without humour. A volume of squibs and parodies could be collected from Whately's "Pastoral Epistle from His Holiness the Pope to some members of the University of Oxford" to the satiric poem of Ronald Knox inscribed "The Absolute and a Bit o' Hell," deriding the Anglican Modernists. The Ingoldsby Legends are chiefly Gothic parodies and figure like gargoyles in the upburst of neo-Catholic writing. A famous Squib was Thomas Longueville's essay on *How to make a Saint,* imagining the canonisation of Laud, Dr. Johnson, and Hannah More to fill gaps in the Anglican Calendar, while Tate and Brady were joined to St. Cecilia! Another skit of Longueville's parodied a Church Congress, at which one of the speakers proposed inter-communion with the Head-Hunters of Borneo, belauding Islam and finding excuses for Polygamy: which inspired Ronald Knox in later days to satirise the craze for Re-union in a pamphlet *Reunion all Round,* in which he suggested including Mahometans, Jews, and Papists even in the Church of England. His headings spoke for themselves:

Heresies and Schisms Very Desirable

Proposal for a Symphorodox Church

A Proposal for Universal Bigamy!

A new Hierarchy was mooted to include Pashas amongst Bishops and Mullahs with Rural Deans. Mahomet was found to be a good and sound Protestant. The inclusion of the Roman clergy offered some difficulty, since their Orders were not null and void, but they could be degraded a step all round and the Pope himself allowed to rank as a retired Missionary Bishop. As for the Cardinals: "I would disperse among the common rooms of Oxford and Cambridge where they would exercise to the full their talent for intrigue without any serious effect."

"The Absolute and a Bit o' Hell" was a direct parody of Dryden's poem "Absolom and Achitophel." Happy the

Church that can produce and receive such exquisite yet classical humour. The approach to the Oxford Movement is thus described in history:

"So Freedom reigned: so Priests dismayed by naught
  Thought what they pleased and mentioned what
    they thought.
Three hundred years and still the land was freed
And Bishops still and Judges disagreed,
Till men began for some account to call
What we believed or why believed at all."

The school of Bishop Gore:

"*Lux Mundi* came and here was found indeed
  A maximum and Minimum of Creed."

The effect of the Higher Critics:

"First Adam fell, then Noah's Ark was drowned
And Samson, under close inspection bound.
For Daniel's blood the Critic lions roared
And trembling hands threw Jonah overboard."

Perhaps the four best lines ever written in religious satire.

VI. THE REACTION ON THE CATHOLIC CHURCH IN ENGLAND

The Tractarians at first raised neither hope nor charity amongst the old English Catholics. It is none the less an interesting piece of History to trace the ensuing effects of the Church of England upon the Church in England; to make the verbal distinction between Roman and Anglican. The English Catholics regarded the High Churchmen as often insincere and wilfully hypocrite, if indeed they took any notice at all. The old dominant State Church they respected. Wiseman arriving at Oscott College, in 1840, from Rome took a sympathetic line towards Oxford. No one who has not been an Anglican can understand Anglicans. Wiseman met them with an inspired wisdom and, though his efforts were scorned by the old Catholics and discouraged by converts, he was equally ready to encourage a Church as he was to catch individuals. Enthusiasts like Pugin and Ambrose De Lisle added their dreams to his and brought him into touch with the Tractarians. Wiseman believed the Oxford Movement was of God and that the Tractarians were sincere. They could not have asked more of their great antagonist and they respected and trusted him. By his comparison of their plight with that of the Donatists he was able to make many think for the first time of surrender to Rome. He refused to believe "that there was no more vitality in the Movement than there was in the time of Laud or of the Nonjurors."

Wiseman allowed De Lisle to intrigue with the Oxford men in his conviction that the conversion of England was wrapped up in their Movement. His fellow-Catholics did not think the conversion of England possible or were little enthused for it. Dr. Russell of Maynooth shared his belief in Newman's sincerity and as a reward they shared his conversion. Wiseman made Oscott a guesthouse and even a lodestar to Oxford men whether they became Catholics or not. Hither came Pugin and Newman, O'Connell and Gladstone, Lord Shrewsbury and Father Mathew, as well as the first converts, Fathers Spencer and Bernard Smith, until Lord Acton as a pupil recalled that "we had a feeling that Oscott, next to Pekin, was a centre of the world." It is important to stress this period, for at the mid-century, between 1845 and 1855, England was nearer if possible to conversion than at any time before or since. Wiseman alone of the Catholics realised the Time Spirit. Oxford Dons like Ward, Oakeley, and Sibthorpe appeared at Oscott. Sibthorpe hung like a leaf on the edge of the gale. Thrice in his dreadful uncertainty he changed religion, but finally for Rome.

Even after the conversion of Newman and his followers, Wiseman received no credit or help from the Old Catholics. They could not perceive that he had taken an isolated and unknown seminary in the Midlands and made it a well-head for the only running current in English Thought. Rome has a wider outlook and little as the Cardinals understood the undercurrents at Oxford, they were aware of strange stirrings that deserved better than disparagement and contempt. Needless to say that when the Pope wished to revive an English Hierarchy it was the English Cardinal Acton *in Curia* who opposed. But Rome has a gift of political second sight for which the faithful have a more exalted term and finding herself distracted between the contrary reports of Wiseman and the Old Catholics, the Holy See recalled her brilliant ambassador to receive the Red Hat and the leadership of the new Hierarchy. She had chosen the right man to make the start.

The English Catholics were a minished and dispirited community. The Irish had only begun to invade England. In moated granges and behind crumbling walls the remnants of old intermarried families brooded over their pedigrees and relics and in high-panelled attics or secret Chapels the Mass was said by family tutors or passing Priests. The Premier Duke and the Premier Earl (Norfolk and Shrewsbury) still held the Faith. Even at times their devotions were musty, for Shrewsbury rose to his feet when his chaplain began reciting the new-fangled Litany of Loretto. In the middle of the century the only Image of Our Lady in London was in St. Mary's Chelsea. Converts were regarded with a doubtful joy. Their enthusiasm seemed perilous and distressing. Lord Stourton suffered "emotions of painful feeling" when he observed the Madonna over the columns of the *Tablet*. The Jesuit Provincial seriously proposed that Newman's followers should help the Apostolate in Timbuctoo. In which case (to revive the famous rhyme) they would have been rid of such enthusiasts as Faber with his Hymn-book too! Faber's Hymns and devotions were found to be sugary and Italian. His *Lives of the Saints* caused even deeper alarm and his treatment of St. Rose of Lima brought suppression to the Series. He could only write: "No sneer of man can wither the marvelous blooming of her leaves: but he will find a thorn who shall dare handle roughly this sweet mysterious Rose which St. Dominic planted in the Garden of his Master." Only a convert could have written thus at this period.

Many of the old families were wavering. Others were dying out. The Earldoms of Huntly and Sefton had apostatised. Pugin's magnificent patron proved to be the last Catholic Earl of Shrewsbury and the Duke of Norfolk, who allowed his daughter to marry Lord Foley in the Chapel Royal, announced his conversion to the State Church at the time of the "Papal Aggression." His son resigned his Parliamentary seat for Arundel and sought a more congenial berth from O'Connell in Ireland.

The national upheaval against Papal Aggression was caused less by the Pope's Bull restoring an English Hierarchy than by the flaming argument of Wiseman and the bitter suspicions roused by the Puseyites. England was then intensely religious or interested in religion, and Wiseman's brilliant Appeal to the English People reached the entire reading public red-hot. Then if ever seemed the chance for Providence. A second wave of converts arrived, headed by Archdeacon Manning, but the antipathy died down with the years. Wiseman even became a popular character. As people became tolerant or indifferent, the mighty rush of conversion, of which Wiseman had dreamed, became more and more remote.

In the rôle of Cardinal, Wiseman lost touch with Oxford and the High Churchmen. He found himself rebuilding the walls of Jerusalem with converts and Old Catholics at variance under him. He found himself struggling with the questions of the new Irish in thousands and the newly installed Religious Orders, who, weak in number and interpreting their rules literally, did not sufficiently assist him. The wide growth of the latter was largely due to converts, who sought the higher vocations and wished to avoid troubles with the old Clergy. They afforded Wiseman inadequate help in the parishes or slums. His long and bitter cry to Faber in 1852 is the most historical document in Purcell's *Life of Manning*. The bitterness between converts and the old guard came to a crisis in Wiseman's own household. The weakening and desponding Cardinal relied more and more on Manning, whose activity and vigilance were devoted to the Cardinal's policy and on the way dislodged Archbishop Errington from his right of succession. The famous story has been told many times: by Purcell, by Lytton Strachey, and by Abbot Butler. Errington's removal by Papal decree was the triumph of the converts over the situation. Rome, judging the conflict of men who were fiercely and equally convinced, extracted her ultimate success by appointing Manning Archbishop in Wiseman's stead.

In Errington the Old Catholics hailed a representative of iron, a man, who could have taken a fleet into the gates of death without flinching. He administered Canon Law with mechanical heartlessness. He was disposed to keep converts in their place and bitterly opposed the Oblates of St. Charles, whom Manning had introduced not only into Westminster Diocese but into St. Edmund's Seminary, the stronghold of the old-fashioned and Gallican tradition. A most indiscreet and impudent convert, Mgr. Talbot, had become the close confidant of the Pope in matters regarding the English and a power behind the throne. The Roman Tribunals gave judgments on the Oblates and the old Colleges in favour of the Bishops against Wiseman and Manning. But the Pope himself removed Errington from the succession at Wiseman's wishes and Talbot's unceasing insistence. Manning had no part in the intrigue beyond stiffening the exhausted Cardinal. When Wiseman died and the Chapter of Westminster chose Errington, Manning only prayed and worked for the translation of Ullathorne from Birmingham. Once again the supreme power was exerted and this time Manning was promoted to the Archbishopric. Errington's vindication appears in Abbot Butler's *Life of Ullathorne* whence two extreme statements may be garnered towards an estimate of his character. There was the current belief that he was willing for souls to go to Hell provided they went by rule: and there is the story of his humble submission "which will scarcely find its parallel except in the lives of God's canonised servants." Errington was God's Englishman all over.

Gladstone kept converts back on the grounds that: (1) The Papacy mixed the human and divine; (2) Pope Honorius was condemned at the Council of Chalcedon for defining heresy; (3) Pascal had shown up the Jesuits.

The Honorius controversy was much laboured during the Vatican Council, in which High Churchmen took a deep interest. Gladstone's views were practically represented there by Lord Acton, who inspired and informed the Gallicans opposing the Infallibility. Acton used the Honorius argument for all its historical value. The answer was that Honorius had been mistaken but not heretical. It appeared that he had talked rubbish *ex tempore* but not *ex cathedra*.

It was a great disappointment to Reunionists that no Anglican Bishops were invited to the Vatican Council. Perhaps it was as well, because the Oxford Movement had not yet accomplished that astonishing change which the Nineteenth Century saw in their enlightenment and spirituality. There were still many of the type whom Baring Gould ridiculed in his *Church Revival:* Hinds of Norwich, who resigned after marrying his cook; Villiers of Carlisle, who presented his best living to his son-in-law (it is true that the subsequent caricature in *Punch* killed both the Bishop and nepotism amongst the Bishops); Baring of Durham, who was only prevented by the Dean from putting Mrs. Baring on the throne beside him. Baring Gould describes Processions, in one of which the episcopal couple appeared under one umbrella, and another in which they followed devotedly if not devoutly in a cab. Dr. Neale described Ordination by the Bishop of Winchester in 1841; a Procession "leading in the Bishopess" for whom the High Churchmen present declined to rise. The Bishop himself was dignified by liveried servants and the Order of the Garter, but it was the Bishopess who intoned the *Veni Creator*. This was Dr. Sumner who owed his whole promotion to being tutor to the mistress of George IV, a fact omitted in his Biography.

Such men would have been out of place in a Church Council, but their successors such as Stubbs, Wordsworth, Lightfoot, Creighton would have added distinction to any religious assembly in history.

The Council was not unaffected by the Oxford Movement owing to the different parts played by Newman and Manning at Rome. On the other hand, the Dogma of Infallibility had the same clearing effect upon Catholics and Anglo-Catholics in England as once the Pope's Bull against Elizabeth. It let all know where they stood, stiffening some towards and others against Rome. Manning's part in whipping and inspiring the Ultramontane Bishops was immense. It was his policy, against the Pope's wish, to place only friends of the Dogma on the all-important Commission *de Fide*. As a result the Minority of Gallicans justly thought they had been excluded and carried on the struggle of opposition from January to July, primed by Acton. Manning was known among the Italians as the "Devil of the Council." Newman, on the other hand, wrote his famous letter, which was "accidentally" published, severely arraigning the extreme party. Pusey was in sympathetic correspondence with Gallicans like Darboy and Doupanloup but his *Eirenicon* was returned by the Roman police. The University of Oxford had the satisfaction of learning that Manning's great speech to the Council was delivered with the Oxford accent.

The converts were naturally inclined to follow the Ultramontanes but there were exceptions like Capes and Richard Simpson, who floated in Acton's historical circle. The English Bishops of the old stock certainly did not favour Manning's impetuous crusade. Ullathorne was the only one definitely not a Gallican. In Manning and Acton the English old Catholics and Oxford converts were represented at their highest power. As far as one man was able, Manning brought about the Definition by informing the British Cabinet and so prevented Gladstone causing intervention by the Powers. Acton had in one way the last word. The famous Letters of Quirinus were written by Döllinger, largely on Acton's inside information. The racy and irresponsible book on the *Infallibility of the Church* by Dr. Salmon of Trinity Dublin, which has supplied the English world with their history of the Council, is based entirely on Quirinus. No impartial or historical account of the Council appeared in English until sixty years afterwards, in Abbot Butler's *Vatican Council,* which would have been equally criticised by Ultramontane and Gallican at the time. It is based on Ullathorne's Letters and it puts both Manning and Acton in their proper places. Gladstone's famous attack on Vaticanism after the Council was answered by Newman enabling Acton to accept the Decrees and to clear himself sufficiently by his letters in the *Times.* He still put Authority above "the authorities": the Church above officials. That Acton escaped the excommunication awarded to Döllinger was due to his confidants among the English Bishops, who, Herbert Paul wrote, "were not sorry to think that the most learned Prelates of the Anglican Church were less learned than a Catholic layman." Manning left Acton to his Bishop: his Bishop left him to the Pope: and the Pope left him alone.

The Oxford Movement had acted as a feeder to the remnant of the old Church. No branch of the Catholic Church in a missionary country has ever received such ready-made assistance or such unhoped encouragement. At the end of the Eighteenth Century Burke estimated there were 30,000 to 36,000 Catholics. In 1840 Archdeacon Manning estimated there were less than a quarter of a million (224,000) Catholics in the country. In the 'Forties came the Irish immigrations owing to the Famine and the numerically smaller flow of University converts. The English Catholics were recruited and refreshed from these twin sources continually, but numbers tell and Manning became aware that he was working for the Irish occupation of England. The Irish brought poverty, cholera, and the Faith with them. Hundreds of missions and Churches scattered throughout England are due to their coming. The Catholic map of England to-day is largely a map of the Irish migrations. In districts they failed to penetrate, such as Wales (except Cardiff), all the West of England, and East Anglia, the Catholic Church only straggles. But Liverpool, Salford, Newcastle, and the North began to breed Irish Ghettos out of which a steady Catholic population slowly ascended the social ladder. In South and East London it was the same. Churches and Schools sprang up wherever Irish flocks had drifted or huddled together. The

Oxford Movement stimulated and adorned the Catholic Revival, but as far as that Revival increased and swelled the Roman Church in England it was due to the Irish. The reverse of the medal was apparent when English of the English found themselves joining "an Irish Church." Tory Tractarians were dismayed by the spectre of O'Connell and later converts were horrified by Fenians, whom Manning and Ullathorne joined in severely discouraging.

Manning's official reign of twenty-seven years laid peace between the converts and the Old Catholics. The opposition rallied themselves, laity and Bishops, behind the name of Newman. Manning was unfortunately driven into hostility to Newman, regarding him as unsafe and dangerous on both doctrine and policy. On the policy of allowing Newman to return to Oxford at the head of an Oratory he was inclined to yield, but he was prejudiced by Ward. In consequence Catholics were not allowed to frequent the Universities. At Oxford Anglicans could breathe again. It is difficult to estimate the result which might have followed Newman's return to the scenes of his dazzling apostolate. He might have influenced a third wave of converts of the Tractarian type. It was his fate to become a minor schoolmaster in a suburb of Birmingham: he who alone had the gift of appealing to the Anglican soul in life or in death.

Converts never ceased, but they were no longer of the old calibre. They were increasing from two thousand to ten thousand a year at the end of the century. In the 'Seventies the Marquesses of Bute and Ripon shook London Society by entering the Church. The former preserved that eccentric cast of intellect which combines superstition with theology and retained his love for astrology and ghostly researches as a Catholic. Lord Ripon converted himself by steeping his mind in Newman and, though he withdrew from politics and the highest Masonic office, he was appointed Viceroy of India. Before he could take office it was necessary to pass the Catholic Disabilities Act, amusingly called the Russell and Ripon Relief Act. Russell of Killowen was a Catholic candidate for Lord Chief Justice of England but Llandaff was the first Catholic to reach the Cabinet. It was typical of his Tory politics that he voted against the Disestablishment of the Anglican Church in Wales and refused to support Russell's and Ripon's Relief because the measure was Mr. Gladstone's. To Protestant alarm he was made Home Secretary.

For one who entered the Catholic Church ten must have found themselves hindered, and in his last years Manning compiled a list of Hindrances under various headings with his opinions attached as a guide to his successors. The first eight of these were published by Purcell: (1) A Clergy neither cultured nor civil; (2) Shallow Preaching; (3) Reaction against Sacred Scripture; (4) Non-perception and unconsciousness of the Spiritual life in England; (5) Sacramentalism, objective and mechanical; (6) Officialism, not subjective; (7) Controversy versus Charity; (8) Dominoes (teaching the Faith in the way dominoes are played). The Ninth Hindrance was the Society of Jesus! and this was not published until it appeared with the approval of the Jesuits in Leslie's *Life of Manning*.

Manning's reign was devoted to practical works. He wrestled with Boards of Guardians, built endless schools, gave London a Seminary and a University College, neither of which survive. He respected the Old Catholics, who served him with loyalty and fear, but he did not scruple to put the Venerable English College at Rome under an Oblate who was also an Irishman. He realised that his strength lay in the Irish, who during his reign outmultiplied English Catholics and converts put together. He allowed his sentiment to become Irish. There are no fixed politics for English Catholics. In Jacobite days they were Tories, but the Whigs gave them Emancipation. To the Whigs they clung until Disraeli drew them back into Toryism and Gladstone by his Home Rule definitely kept them out of the Liberal ranks. But Manning was a democrat at heart and championed not only the Irish but the Labour Cause. His old Evangelical fervour sent him headlong into every social cause of the day, from agricultural labourers to the unfortunates of the street, from antislavery to total abstinence. To the horror and alarm of the Old Catholics he ended his career by settling the great Dock Strike of 1889 single-handed and literally releasing the Thames from stoppage.

Within three years died Manning, Newman, and Ullathorne. Cardinal Vaughan who succeeded came of the old stock, and the careers of the two great convert-Cardinals passed into legend. But Ullathorne had always held his own between Manning and Newman, revered and appreciated by one and unafraid of the other. Although Ward described the difference between the old stock and the converts as that between barbarians and civilised, there are many who believe that the Old Catholics could have revived and adorned their Church out of their own stock even if there had been no Oxford Movement. Under the hardest conditions they had produced Challoner, Milner, and Lingard. Wiseman was the greatest Churchman in Europe after the Pope himself. Ullathorne, who came of the blood of Sir Thomas More, had a dignity and power which could dispense with Oxford manners or degrees. He was a rough diamond like most of Wiseman's Bishops, but the convert Bishops appeared to Old Catholic eyes to be made of Anglican paste. In any case there were no more of them after Manning's reign and the Church in England became more and more what it would have been without the intrusion of the Oxford men. The times called for administrators, not national characters, for business organisers, not brilliant controversialists. Under Cardinal Vaughan the question of Anglican Orders was finally settled and both Churches found that they could unite preferably on the Education Question. They were thrown together in support of their Voluntary Schools and in impassioned and successful defence against the Education Acts of the Liberal Government. In spite of their Passive Resistance, the Dissenters were unable to "put Rome off the Rates." Cardinal Vaughan worked only to consolidate the position of his predecessors. The majestic and abysmal Cathedral of Westminster was completed and converts mingled their offerings with those of the old families, whom Cardinal Vaughan represented with real splendour. Lord Brampton, a convert Judge, put his fortune into one of the Cathedral Chapels. The Catholic advance was slow and not sensational. Missions sprang up all down the line but of a small character. From time to time the Holy See added Provinces of new Archbishoprics, which John Bull disdained to regard as dangerous or aggressive.

Any Catholic advance is generally written about in terms of jubilation or alarm. A scientific enquiry using the coldest and most impartial methods would be of greater value. Churches have shown themselves so shy of religious census since the War that any figures have become suspect. Pious miscalculations in taking the numbers of any religious body are venial, but there is no reason for not accepting the figures supplied by the *Catholic Directory*. They must remain a great satisfaction in the face of the decreasing numbers in other Churches. At the same time scientific enquiry would note the large and persistent leakage in England. The action of local authorities lost an enormous number of Catholic children in the past, which was checked by Cardinals Manning and Vaughan. The presence or absence of a Catholic School made itself felt in the second and third generation. The Catholic School system is perhaps the greatest achievement of the Church in England. Nevertheless, given the great numbers of Irish immigrants who have been coming over for three generations, the surprise is not that there are so many Catholics but that there are so few. It is not that they have failed to multiply, but that for various reasons the issue of their multiplication often passes out of the reach of the Church. Just as a Catholic atmosphere will gradually absorb a non-Catholic element (History has shown again and again in Ireland), poverty, intermarriage, lack of schools and churches has diverted an enormous quantity of Irish blood, seldom into other Churches, but constantly into the indifference of English country life. The soil and atmosphere of England is un-Catholic. Catholicism, both Roman and Anglican, thrives in the towns like the prophet's gourd, but in the agricultural counties it remains a struggling exotic. Given the numbers of Catholic Irish who came during and after the 'Forties, there ought to be four millions of their stock. Possibly there are, but less than a half are Catholic.

The Catholic increase is largely due to the large family which is practised amongst the poor and the Irish. This is the most biting question to-day. Antiquarian and liturgical questions rouse little interest. From Anglican Orders to the Relics of St. Edmund these have been settled. All Churches are faced by the far more difficult problems of population, poverty and unemployment, and by the struggles of Socialism within a disturbed Capitalist State. The population question in its influence on the Catholic Church can be most vividly studied in Scotland, where in a century the Catholics have become an eighth instead of a thirtieth of the country. This is due entirely to the Irish migrations into Glasgow and the industrial towns. As the native Protestant Scotch have been lessened in proportion through various reasons, the situation has become one of obvious alarm to the Protestant Churches. If the proportions are maintained, it is possible to calculate when Scotland like Canada will have a Catholic majority. Let not this possibility be attributed to the Oxford Movement, which has expended its influence in ritualising the Scotch Episcopal Church and in winning a distinguished number of Lairds and Aristocrats, of whom Abbot Hunter Blair built the great Benedictine Monastery of Fort Augustus. If the 600,000 Catholics in Scotland are added to those in England, a surprising result is reached. They outnumber the Catholics in the Irish Free State by 80,000. The Scotch Home Rule agitation has to face the probability of a quarter of the Scotch seats falling under Irish or Catholic influence.

In the self-satisfaction caused by the great Catholic growth the problems underlying the statistics are not often studied. Since Manning made his calculation of "Romanists" in 1840 his number has been multiplied by ten. There are 2,235,000 Catholics in England and Wales. To regard this increase as due to converts or the descendants of converts and made by the Oxford Movement would be ludicrous. In fifty years the number of Priests has doubled from two thousand to four thousand, a number shared to a very small extent by converts. If nomenclature is an indication, the names of the Priests serving in England are largely Irish, though their blood or culture may have often been tempered by English birth. About one thousand Parsons have been converted to Rome since the Oxford Movement commenced. Though Propaganda no longer ministers England as a Missionary country, Ireland in simple practice sends her missionaries to England and China alike. With all its intellectual and artistic issues the Oxford Movement has been played out as an auxiliary to Rome.

Its surviving strength and vitality remain to activate the Church of England. Of the ten to twelve thousand annual conversions, which are claimed by the Roman officials in England, not a tithe are due to the motives which once influenced the Oxford men. They are due to mixed marriages, reaction from Socialism, independent thinking, Anglican confusions, and often to the neighbourhood of a Catholic mission and population. The desire to stand within reach of security in religious and social teaching is the reason which leads most to seek peace with Rome.

The Oxford Movement can certainly claim the recent literary converts. Dean Inge has called attention to his belief that none of them are in the front rank of letters: Compton Mackenzie, Maurice Baring, G. K. Chesterton. Great Statesmen and Theologians come no more, but most years are marked by some such individualist as Ronald Knox, Fr. Vernon, or Dr. Orchard. Dr. Orchard as a Ritualist and a Dissenter was one of the oddest productions of the Oxford Movement. The rivulet of outstanding converts has become a trickle. Early in the Movement conversion seemed a romantic and even perilous step. To-day it is respected as a comfortable and sensible act. Converts no longer become social outcasts but pride themselves on acquiring sturdier citizenship. The Catholic community is a pillar of the English State, though not too kind a step-sister to the State Church. But there is a remote front of civilisation upon which England and the Pope may find themselves allies, in which case the Church of England may follow a hint from the State to accept terms, generous or ungenerous, from Rome.

VII. A SELECT BIBLIOGRAPHY OF THE OXFORD MOVEMENT

DEAN CHURCH: *History of the Oxford Movement.* "Combines the freshness of personal knowledge with a sureness of judgment against which there is no appeal." G. P. Gooch in *Historians of the Nineteenth Century.*

ISAAC WILLIAMS: *Autobiography.* A Tractarian Idyll. Reminiscences of a devout Welsh poet who followed Newman as far as the Rubicon but not across. "The most fascinating record of the time which any of the leaders bequeathed to posterity. In it every phase of the Movement as it appealed to one of the chief disciples is recorded without a touch of exaggeration. It explains the attractiveness of Newman, the devotion of his followers, the sincerity of their principles, the tragedy of their separation." R. H. Hutton in *Cambridge History of English Literature.*

THOMAS MOZLEY: *Reminiscences of the Oxford Movement.* Uncritical but lively anecdotes by Newman's brother-in-law. "If a story cannot stand on two legs, Tom supplies a third." Newman.

MARK PATTISON: *Memoirs.* Embittered retrospect of Oxford politics by one who walked once with Newman and turned back to become Warden of Lincoln.

JOHN HENRY NEWMAN: *Apologia pro vita sua.* "A retreat to military music." Francis Newman. "A voice from the dead." Cardinal Manning. The ablest handbook to the Movement and an exquisite revelation of what Newman thought he once thought after thirty years. A comet retracing its own orbit. As autobiography perhaps the greatest in English. Compared with Augustine's the *Apologia* is written by a Stylist turned Controversialist, as against the Confessions of a Sensualist turned Saint.

W. G. WARD: *The Ideal of a Christian Church*. The Papal Guy with which a logical Tutor stampeded a learned University and caused a breakdown to the Movement.

Lyra Apostolica. Poems chiefly by Newman and Keble and Isaac Williams, the three versifiers of the Movement. Faber, the real poet, omitted.

JOHN KEBLE: *The Christian Year*. Better the Anglican Year by an Anglican Adam of St. Victor.

JAMES FROUDE: *The Nemesis of Faith*.
The Apology of a Relapsed Tractarian. Publicly burnt in the University.

E. B. PUSEY: *Eirenicon*. Three Parts. Olive branches to Rome with more stick than leaf. Olive leaves carried in a raven's beak.

WILFRID WARD: *Life of Cardinal Wiseman*. A vivid and generous survey of the Oxford Movement as it affected an enthusiastic and long-suffering Cardinal. A most interesting chapter in the First Edition was suppressed, presumably by Authority (Chapter XXXI, "The Exclusive Church and the Zeitgeist"). The Appendix endeavours to take the sting out of Purcell's account of the duel between Manning and Errington.

W. G. Ward and the Catholic Revival. "The very singular figure of the English landowner who did not know the difference between wheat and barley and preferred teaching candidates for the Romish Priesthood." Prof. Marcus Dods.

W. G. Ward and the Oxford Movement. These volumes form a monument of filial piety and appear to transfer the leadership of the Movement from Newman to Ward, who was his ape as an Anglican and his persecutor as a Catholic.

The Life of Cardinal Newman. The last word on Newman but not on Newmanism. A finely documented memorial but the scale of failure and unhappiness is unduly pressed. Newman's line of thought against Ward and Manning is sympathetically developed but the relation of Newmanism to Modernism is left untouched.

E. S. PURCELL: *The Life of Cardinal Manning.* "Almost a crime." Cardinal Vaughan. "The greatest and truest of modern biographies." Prof. Bury. "A fascinating tragicomedy." Archbishop Benson.

SHANE LESLIE: *The Life and Labours of Cardinal Manning.*

LYTTON STRACHEY: *Eminent Victorians.* The following Epigram covers the three Lives of Cardinal Manning mentioned above:

>"First Purcell damned him for a hoary
>Hypocrite in double tomes derogatory:
>Then Leslie wrote a laudatory
>Puff to his celestial glory:
>But Lytton Strachey's mild inculpatory
>Was given him to read in Purgatory."

E. S. PURCELL: *The Life of Ambrose Phillips de Lisle.* Indiscreet but historical and well documented as to Wiseman's pious intrigues with the Tractarians and the Reunionists. The papers of a defeated dreamer who fascinated both Wiseman and Gladstone and whom only Time can justify.

REGINALD WILBERFORCE: *Life of Bishop Wilberforce.* "The Sin of Ham." Cardinal Manning. In spite of indiscretions which reveal the Bishop's human hates and feelings the work gives a clear and living picture of what an Anglican Bishop could become when transfigured by the very Movement which he strove to oppose and control.

HODDER: *Life of Lord Shaftesbury.* An insight into the noble social crusades of the last Evangelical Leader, illumined by his lurid and apocalyptic Protestantism.

CANON LIDDON: *Life of Pusey.* A doctrinal and documental monument under which Pusey lies buried and as yet unexcavated. Is it the fate of a Heresiarch to be buried under the rubbish of his own temple?

LORD IRWIN: *John Keble.* A sincere and unexciting account of the retiring country parson, who set the first match to the flame of the Oxford Movement, by a Viceroy of India, who has the greater distinction of being a son of Lord Halifax.

DR. DAVIDSON: *Life of Archbishop Tait.* A fair account of how the Ritualists were fought and incidentally proving that an Archbishop can be a hero to his Chaplain.

A. C. BENSON: *Life of Archbishop Benson.* A literary and impartial account of the High Church Primate by his son in a vein of agnostic Anglicanism. Discreet and discerning. Valuable for the inside history of the Lincoln Judgment and the official attitude to the Roman Commission on Anglican Orders.

J. H. POLLEN: *Five Years at St. Saviour's Leeds.* A heartbreaking account of the first Tractarian mission to the industrial North amid scenes of vile corruption and cholera. Typical of many such since but the most pathetic. Pusey was not allowed to call his Church after the Holy Cross nor to inscribe the Chalice with a prayer for his dead child.

C. E. OSBORNE: *The Life of Father Dolling.* An Anglican Vincent de Paul painted in glowing colours.

ABBOT BUTLER: *The Life of Archbishop Ullathorne.* From cabin-boy to Archbishop. Perhaps the greatest Englishman ever to go to Australia. The finest and most impartial Biography the Oxford Movement has produced. Gives the case of Errington as against Manning and Wiseman and trims the balance tidily between Wiseman and the Old Catholics.

J. SNEAD-COX: *Life of Cardinal Vaughan.* Invaluable for the Chapter on Lambeth and Anglican Orders. A biography which should worry the *Advocatus Diaboli* considerably.

J. W. BOWDEN: *Life of Faber.* Contains interesting correspondence but reads like a great chance missed. A glowing poet reduced to poor prose. The true Life of Faber is yet to be written and leaves a real gap in the history of the Movement: especially his conflict with Newman.

MISS PETRE: *Autobiography and Life of Father Tyrrell.* The first volume written by Tyrrell explains and an-

swers the second written in defence of his Modernism.
The Autobiography is a painful but fascinating piece of
self-probing. A self-stinging hornet.

C. C. MARTINDALE: *Life of Robert Hugh Benson.* A fine
exposition of Benson's literary wares and personality.

R. A. KNOX: *A Spiritual Ænead.* A *sors Virgiliana,* which
drew Rome! The gulf between the Tractarian and the
modern Anglo-Catholic can be measured by compar-
ing the Apologies of the two convert members of Trinity: Newman and Knox.

(ANGLICAN ORDERS)

LE COURAYER: *Validité des Ordinations Anglicanes,* 1723.

LE QUIEN: *Nullité des Ordinations Anglicanes,* 1725. Gallican Priests writing for or against. Le Courayer was
condemned by the Pope and translated by the Tractarians.

CANON ESTCOURT: *The Question of Anglican Ordinations.*
Though written from the Roman side, contains the sup-
posed decree of 1704 assimilating Anglican with Abys-
sinian Orders, which the Holy See recognised. This was
corrected by Rome writing to Cardinal Manning in
1875.

A. S. BARNES: *The Popes and the Ordinal.* A collection of
the essential documents by an antiquarian, whose detective powers have been exercised on the man in the Iron
Mask and the site of St. Peter's body.

Cardinal Gasquet and Edmund Bishop. *Edward VI and
the Book of Common Prayer.* A powerful combination
of experts dissecting the First and Second Prayer Books

and leaving them in naked comparison with the Sarum rite. Edmund Bishop was one of the great liturgical minds thrown up by the Oxford Movement. He lived with the Benedictines and his formidable scholarship lay behind Cardinal Gasquet's pen.

CANON LACEY: *De Re Anglicana.* The Anglican Case scholarly and brilliant enough to have won the admiration if not the consent of the Cardinals in 1896.

VIII. MAP OF THE OXFORD MOVEMENT

CANTERBURY	OXFORD (High Church)	ROME
Archbp. Cranmer		Cardinal Pole
Bp. Barlow		Stapleton
	(Anglican Martyrs)	
Archbishop Parker	Archbp. Laud	Fr. Sancta Clara
	Charles I	(Davenport)
	(Nonjurors)	
	Archbp. Sancroft	
	Bp. Ken	
	Chas. Leslie	
	Dr. Sacheverell	Milner
(Low Church)	(Tractarians)	Lingard
Archbp. Howley	Keble	Cardinal Wiseman
Dr. Arnold	Pusey	Bp. Ullathorne
	Newman	
Ld. Shaftesbury	Froude	
	Pattison	
(Broad Church)		
Bp. Hampden		
Gorham		
Dean Stanley		
Bp. Colenso	Faber	Lord Acton
(Essays and Re-views)	Coffin → Bp.	
Jowett		
Archbp. Temple		

Kingsley

Patterson ——————→ Bp.
Wilkinson ——————→ Bp.
Ward ———————→
Gladstone
Hope Scott ——————→
Manning ———————→
Archd. Wilberforce ——————→

Bp. Wilberforce ——————→
(*Ritualists*)
Bennett
Prynne
Neale
Mackonochie
Fr. Ignatius
Bp. King
Lord Halifax ——————→ Cardinal Vaughan

Archbp. Benson
(*Anglo-Catholics*)
Dean Liddon
Fr. Dolling
Bp. Gore

Archbp. Tait

Sir Wm. Harcourt

Archbp. Davidson

(*Modernists*)

Bp. Weston
R. H. Benson ——————→
G. K. Chesterton ——————→ Fr. Tyrrell
Von Hugel

Ld. Brentford

Dean Inge
Bp. Barnes